WOMEN'S PROGRAMS FOR EVERY SEASON

MATILDA
NORDTVEDT
AND PEARL
STEINKUEHLER

MOODY PRESS
THE NAME YOU CAN TRUST

CHICAGO, ILLINOIS

Library of Congress Cataloging in Publication Data

Nordtvedt, Matilda.
 Women's programs for every season.

 Includes bibliographical references.
 1. Worship programs. 2. Women—Religious life.
I. Steinkuehler, Pearl. II. Title.
BV199.W6N65   265′.9   82-6391
ISBN 0-8024-6903-5   AACR2

4 5 6 7 Printing/LC/Year 89 88 87 86

Printed in the United States of America

Contents

1
Programs with a Purpose

Women are very special creations of God. They are creatures of beauty, and they greatly appreciate beautiful things. They respond to ideas and objects that appeal to their senses. Capitalize upon those qualities as you enter into your women's programs.

It would be a sin to do any of God's work in a boring, humdrum fashion. Work hard to prevent offending any woman's senses or sensibilities by presenting to her a shoddy, poorly prepared program.

Discover the abilities of your women and prospective members, and offer them opportunities to use those talents in God's service. Involve as many women and their varied abilities as possible. Art, music, drama, craft skills, and culinary arts all add much to create a program that continues to change lives long after the final "amen."

A good program contains these three elements: inspiration, information, and opportunity for expression. Inspiration without expression leads to depression. In preparing each program, ask, "What difference will this make to us?" Build every activity around your chosen theme. Decorations and refreshments should also be in keeping with the theme. To evaluate the finished product, determine, "What do we do now that we know and feel a need?" Check results to see if anything of value is being accomplished.

We offer the following programs for your use as is, or modified by you to best meet your group's needs. They are organized by months, with an added chapter to help you make programs of your own. Feel free to adapt, update, or personalize the ideas to reach the maximum number of women for the deepest commitment to the Lord.

No plain Jane programs, please!

2
January

GOD'S WORD FOR THE NEW YEAR

Opening Song: "Thy Word Is Like a Garden, Lord"

Leader: The month of January was named for Janus, the ancient Roman god of beginnings. Janus had two faces so that he could look backward and forward at the same time. It was believed that Janus could not only evaluate the old year, but also perceive what would happen in the new one.[*]

We realize that only our all-knowing God knows what the new year holds. What will take place in our government? in our homes? in our schools? at our jobs?

The new year is an unknown and untried path. "You have not passed this way before," said the officers of the Israelites to the people when they were about to cross the Jordan River into the promised land. Neither have we passed through the days and months of the coming year.

We have a map for our journey through this new year, however. It is the Word of God. Only by God's directions as given to us in His Word can we know how to live successfully. Only by God's promises can we obtain the courage and strength we need for the days and months that lie before us.

---

[*]*Deluxe Personal Appointment Book* (Woodbury, N.Y.: Bobley, 1979), p. 35.

Let's open our Bibles to Psalm 119. *(Assign the different sections of the psalm to your women. They may work singly or in pairs. After about ten minutes, have the women report to you their findings under two categories: "How did the psalmist feel about God's Word?" and "What does God's Word do for us?" Write on a chalkboard or large sheet of paper.)*

HOW DID THE PSALMIST FEEL ABOUT GOD'S WORD?

Rejoiced in it (v. 14)

Longed for it (v. 40)

Believed it (v. 66)

Delighted in it (v. 70)

Meditated on it all the day (v. 97)

Loved it (v. 97)

 better than thousands of gold and silver (v. 72)

 as sweeter than honey (v. 103)

 as the rejoicing of his heart (v. 111)

 as finding great spoil (v. 162)

WHAT DOES GOD'S WORD DO FOR ME?

Cleanses me (v. 9)

Keeps me from sin (v. 11)

Delights me (v. 24)

Counsels me (v. 24)

Strengthens me (v. 28)

Gives me liberty (v. 45)

Gives me hope (v. 49)

Gives me comfort (v. 50)

Gives me life (v. 50)

Gives me a song (v. 54)

Is my wisdom (vv. 98, 100)

Is a lamp unto my feet (v. 105)

Sustains me (v. 116)

Gives me light (v. 130)

Revives me (v. 156)

Gives me peace (v. 165)

Leader: Do we feel about God's Word as the psalmist did? Or have we neglected its treasures to our own impoverishment? Look what it can do for us! Do you need cleansing, counsel, strength, hope, comfort, and peace? Do you need wisdom and direction for the new year? It's all here in God's Word. The problem is, how do we find time in our busy lives to search out this treasure and make it our own? We will now have a panel of ladies to discuss that topic. Those of you in the audience may feel free to ask questions or offer your own suggestions.

Panel: "God's Word in My Life in the Coming Year"

(When choosing members for any panel discussion, select women who are born-again and who read their Bibles regularly. Always show prospective members the list of questions beforehand. That will give them a chance to think through the questions. Also, those women not qualified or comfortable can then ask to be excused from participating. Try to include women of different ages and from different backgrounds.)

1. What does God's Word mean to me?
   Instances when God has met your need through a specific portion or verse *(encourage audience participation here.)*
2. When shall I read and study the Bible?
   How to fit a quiet time into your busy schedule
   What about interruptions?
3. What about Bible studies with others?
   Church, neighborhood, family
4. What about memorization and meditation?
   Possibilities of doing this while working at household tasks, driving, and so on
5. Suggest a workable plan for Bible reading in the new year for a busy homemaker or a working mother.
6. What are the rewards?
   Strength, hope, optimism, seeing things from God's perspective, cleansing, wisdom, and so on

Silent Prayer: Encourage women to talk to God about letting His Word have a more prominent place in their lives during the coming year.

Songs: "Wonderful Words of Life"
  "Standing on the Promises"

INSTALLATION OF OFFICERS

An installation of new officers may be as elaborate or as simple as you desire. Even a short ceremony is impressive if an object lesson is used in the challenge. Two ideas are given here: one very brief and the other longer and more elaborate.

LEADERS LIGHT THE WAY

Prepare a poster of this acrostic. Place it on a stand in center front. Provide a pastel candle for each outgoing officer. Ask outgoing leaders to stand to the speaker's right, and incoming officers to stand to the left when called.

L . . . oyal to Christ and the church
E . . . ncourages others
A . . . lert to needs around us
D . . . edicates efforts and abilities to the Lord
E . . . nrolls in training opportunities
R . . . ecognizes the need for prayer and meditation

PROGRAM

Speaker: Jesus told His followers, "I am the light of the world; he who follows Me shall not walk in the darkness, but shall have the light of life" (John 8:12). He also said: "You are the light of the world. A city set on a hill cannot be hidden. Nor do men light a lamp, and put it under the peck-measure, but on the lampstand; and it gives light to all who are in the house. Let your light shine before men in such a way that they may see your good works, and glorify your Father who is in heaven" (Matthew 5:14-16). Our leaders serve as lights to illuminate the way of walking with the Lord of light. We have had a good set of officers who exhibited outstanding qualities of leadership. Will our outgoing officers please stand? (*Leaders stand with lighted candles at speaker's right.*)

Speaker: Each of these ladies has been (*read statements on the acrostic poster*). Each has carried well the light of leadership. (*to leaders*) Thank you for showing the way. Will the incoming officers please stand on my left? (*Incoming officers stand.*) We now transfer the light of leadership to you. (*Outgoing leaders give their candles to their respective incoming officers and then sit down.*)

Speaker: (*to new leaders*) We challenge you to pattern your leadership after the qualities charted before you. Leaders are powerless unless they have loyal followers. We stand to pledge ourselves to uphold you in prayer and follow your leadership. (*People stand. Speaker continues speaking.*) We are all admonished in Ephesians 5:8-10: "Now you are light in the Lord; walk as children of light (for the fruit of the light consists in all goodness and righteousness and truth), trying to learn what is pleasing to the Lord." (*to leaders*) Will you accept the mantle of leadership we offer you? (*Officers answer in unison, "I will."*) We pray, to dedicate you and ourselves to the Lord's service.

Prayer of Dedication

ACTIONS SPEAK LOUDER THAN WORDS

In this installation service, the responses of the officers are in actions, not words. A rehearsal will be needed to assure gracefulness as officers stand during the speaker's comments and together assume indicated poses during songs.

Participants needed are a speaker who installs the officers, the incoming officers, and a soloist or vocal group. Officers should dress in similar apparel or wear choir robes. Singers stand in an inconspicuous place and sing the first stanza and chorus of suggested songs or other appropriate ones, unannounced, at the proper times. If there will be deaf people in attendance, select an interpreter to sign the entire commitment service.

Prepare a printed program listing the order of service, the officers' names and titles, and the program participants.

Stage setting should be simple, with candles or a spotlight focusing on the front and the auditorium darkened. As the service begins, the officers stand in a line facing the audience, with the speaker at their right.

11

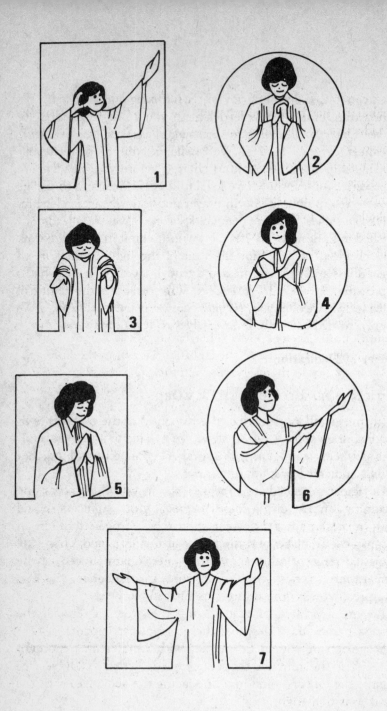

12

Speaker: It has been said through the years that actions speak louder than words. The officers you elected to serve you this year have decided to let actions speak for their commitment to serving God and you. They will use sign language to show their acceptance of the responsibilities you have placed upon their shoulders. * They have not arrived at this sense of dedication quickly, nor do they take their responsibilities lightly. They first listened to the voice of God, and like the boy Samuel in the Old Testament, they answer, "Speak, for Thy servant is listening" (1 Samuel 3:10b).

(Pose 1. The right hand is cupped behind the right ear. The left arm and hand are extended upward toward the left front, and the head is lifted slightly in the direction of the left arm.)

Hymn: "Lord, Speak to Me, That I May Speak"

Speaker: Their response to the call to service from the Lord and you is to clothe themselves in humility. *(Read 1 Peter 5:6-7.)*

(Pose 2. Cup the right hand over the closed left hand in an attitude of prayer at about chin level, and bow the head.)

Hymn: "I Am Thine, O Lord"

Speaker: These, your officers, have tried to empty their hearts of all selfish desires and unworthy motives. They seek to surrender completely to the will of God.

(Pose 3. Extend arms with open hands, palms down, in front of body, slightly above waist level, and bow the head.)

Hymn: "All to Jesus I Surrender"

Speaker: These women commit themselves to love God and all people. *(Read John 15:12 and 1 John 3:18.)*

(Pose 4. Cross wrists, hands open, across breast, head slightly raised, with eyes turned upward.)

Hymn: "I Love Thee"

---

*Sign language taken from Nicy Murphy, "Life Changing Commitments," *Dimension*, October-November-December 1979. Used by permission of Woman's Missionary Union.

Speaker: They know their limitations, so they commit themselves to prayer. They pray for themselves, this organization they lead, and the lost and needy people of the world.

(Pose 5. Clasp palms of hands together in front of chest in an attitude of prayer, and bow the head.)

Hymn: "Sweet Hour of Prayer"

Speaker: *(Read Philippians 4:13.)* Your elected leaders know that their strength comes from God. They seek to serve God through the varied facets of this organization.

(Pose 6. Arms and hands are outstretched in front of the body, palms up, with the left hand slightly in front of the right.)

Hymn: "Take My Life, Lead Me Lord"

Speaker: Your officers realize that their service goes far beyond the limits of this church. They seek to guide you to embrace the world and its needs by praying, giving, and going.

(Pose 7. Arms are slightly bent and held spread apart in front of the body, as if embracing a globe.)

Hymn: "We've a Story to Tell"

Speaker: The actions of our officers speak beautifully of their commitment to serve God and you through love, prayer, and service. Does their commitment stir you to like actions? Should their commitment be any greater than yours? We all serve the same God.

If you are willing to work with these officers and commit yourselves to the Lord's service, please stand and sing from memory your pledge with the words of the first verse and chorus of "Take My Life, and Let It Be."

Prayer of Dedication

3

February

NOTHING SAYS LOVING . . . (BANQUET)

Promote this as a program for single people as well as couples.

Carry out a "chef" theme in decorations. Use red- and white-checkered tablecloths and red and white candles. Arrange on each table a stand-up "chef" (made of cardboard or other heavy material according to the pattern provided) and an empty spice jar (as a vase) with miniature children's cooking utensils fastened to chenille stems interspersed with a few small, artificial flowers and hearts on chenille stems.

Buy red or white nut cups, and stand up in them, among the nuts and heart candies, paper chef's hats (made according to sketch provided), which also serve as place cards with the guest's name written under "CHEF." Put in each nut cup a proverb (see list below) to be read by each guest when called for.

PROGRAM

Prayer of Table Blessing

Dinner

Special Music (a medley of love songs sung by a soloist, vocal group, or barbershop quartet)

Speaker: A popular commercial says, "Nothing says loving like something from the oven." Those are wise words, indeed. We have enjoyed a lot of goodies from the stove and the oven tonight. Other

15

wise words, often called proverbs, are hidden in your nut cups. Would you retrieve yours and read the words of wisdom? When you read yours, please identify it, if you can, as biblical wisdom or man's wisdom. *(Hear proverbs from all, going around each table in turn.)*

Reading of the Proverbs

Speaker: We have heard much wisdom tonight. Love from the oven tastes great but is not always good for us. It affects some of us adversely and adds inches to the waist if we enjoy too much of that kind of loving! The very best kind of love is God's kind of love as revealed in the Bible. *(Read 1 Corinthians 13.)* This is love in action, love that lasts and lasts, love that brings only good to the giver and to the recipient of the love. Let us seek to pattern our love life after God's directions and example.

Prayer of Dismissal

Proverbs (One in each nut cup. Biblical proverbs are marked with an asterisk.)

The way to a man's heart is through his stomach.
A soft answer turns away wrath. *
A wise woman builds her house. *
Pride goes before destruction, and a haughty spirit before a fall. *
A stitch in time saves nine.
Early to bed, early to rise, makes a man healthy, wealthy, and wise.
A penny saved is a penny earned.
Absence makes the heart grow fonder.
Waste not, want not.
Who the daughter would win, with Mama must begin.
Don't put all your eggs in one basket.
Pretty is as pretty does.
Beauty is only skin deep.
Actions speak louder than words.
Don't count your chickens before they hatch.
A bird in hand is worth two in the bush.
Cleanliness is next to godliness.
The fear of the Lord is the beginning of wisdom. *

17

A wise son makes a father glad. *

The memory of the righteous is blessed. *

As a ring of gold in a swine's snout, so is a beautiful woman who lacks discretion. *

He who spares the rod hates his son. *

There is a way that seems right to a man, but its end is the way of death. *

Better is a dish of vegetables where love is, than a fattened ox and hatred with it. *

A gray head is a crown of glory. *

A friend loves at all times, and a brother is born for adversity. *

He who finds a wife finds a good thing. *

A good name is to be more desired than great riches. *

Train up a child in the way he should go, and when he is old he will not depart from it. *

LOVE STORY (BANQUET)

Again, promote this as an event for both singles and couples. Meet at a restaurant, or prepare a meal in the church parlor.

PROGRAM

Prayer of Table Blessing
Dinner
Game: Call three couples to the front. Send the three men out of the room. Ask the women the following questions. (*Someone with paper and pencil should record each woman's answer.*)

1. Do you tell your husband how to drive?
2. What did your husband say when he proposed?
3. What is your husband's pet name for you?
4. What is your pet name for him?
5. How many times a day do you tell him you love him?
6. What is your husband's pet peeve?
7. What is your husband's favorite meal?
8. What is your husband's favorite color?

18

9. How often does your husband buy you flowers?

10. What does your husband think of your family?

When the three wives have answered all the questions, bring in the three husbands and ask them the same questions, in turn: "Does your wife tell you how to drive?" and so on. Give a point to the husband when his answer agrees with his wife's. The couple with the most points at the end wins a small prize.

How They Met: Ask three people to tell how they met their mates (*time limit: three minutes each*).

Leader: We have heard these love stories with much interest. "All the world loves a lover" and enjoys hearing about dreams and hopes fulfilled in a happy marriage.

There is another kind of love story, however, that is even more important and thrilling—God's love for us as demonstrated in His sending His Son to be our Savior. (*Read or quote John 3:16 and 1 John 4:10.*) Now we will hear how several of our friends met Christ and experienced His great love.

Testimonies:

(*Note: You may want only one longer testimony instead of several short ones.*)

Closing Song: "Jesus, Lover of My Soul"

4
March

BIRTHDAY PARTY

Do you need to raise money for a missionary project? Why not put on a birthday party for the entire church? Beforehand, contact two or three missionaries who have birthdays in the month of March (or in whatever month you use this program). Ask them to write a short letter of greeting to be read at the meeting. Be sure they include at least one prayer request.

PROGRAM

Congregational Singing: "Sweeter as the Years Go By"
Missionary Birthdays: Read letters from missionaries.

        Have several prayers for missionaries.

        Light candles on a birthday cake, blow them out, and sing "Happy Birthday, Dear Missionaries."

        Explain that the offering will go for a missionary project.

Scripture Reading: John 3:1-7, 16-17
Solo: "The Longer I Serve Him"
Film: "Born Again" (about Charles Colson) *or*
Testimonies: by local Christians about how they came to Christ. Be sure to include not only dramatic testimonies, but also nondramatic ones that people can relate to who were converted as children.

20

After the above program, retire to the church parlor for the party. Each table should be decorated for a month of the year: January, snowman; February, hearts; March, shamrock; April, Easter decorations; May, flowers; June, bride doll; July, flags; August, toy recreational vehicles; September, schoolbooks, crayons, pencils; October, pumpkins, produce; November, Pilgrims and horn of plenty; December, Christmas decorations. If your group is small, use six tables instead of twelve, with two months represented by each, putting the decorations on the ends instead of in the center.

The guests will eat at the table representing their birthday month and put their offering in the receptacle provided on the table for that purpose. This is a good way to get people to talk to others besides their own particular friends.

Serve a large, decorated birthday cake and ice cream, or have a cake on each table with candles to blow out. Don't forget multicolored balloons hanging from the ceiling to make it look like a real party. Sing "Happy Birthday to Everybody."

Spring Cleaning

Decorate with cleaning articles: mops, brooms, dusters, boxes of cleanser, and so on.

PROGRAM

Song: "When It's Springtime in the Rockies"
Skit: "Millie's Lament," by Kathy Shiffer
    Characters: Clara, dowdy, middle-aged cleaning woman in an office building. Millie, also a cleaning woman, absent-minded and clumsy
    Setting: One room of an office building after office hours. There are mops, brooms, buckets, and feather dusters strewn about.

21

(The scene opens with Clara on stage by herself. She is mopping the floor diligently, pausing at times to look toward the place where Millie will enter.)

Clara: Sure has been a long night. I ain't never gonna git out of here 'less Millie shows up pretty soon to help me finish this room. Wonder what could be keepin' her? Should have been done with the rooms in her end of the buildin' long ago. *(Looks up, smiles brightly.)* Well, there's the ol' girl now! *(Enter Millie, carrying an assortment of pails, brooms, mops, and so on. All along the way, she drops sponges and cleaning rags. She stoops to pick them up, dropping other items in the process.)*

Millie: Sorry I'm late, hon. I got here jest as fast as I could, but you know me. My land sakes honey, you've jest about got the place all spic and span already! *(As she says this, she turns around full circle to look and nearly whacks Clara with the broom and mop handles. Clara jumps out of the way just in time.)* I'm so sorry to leave you with all the work like this. Well now, where shall I start? *(She looks around, nearly whacking Clara with the broom handles again.)*

Clara: *(shakily)* Well, dear, why don't you just begin by emptyin' them wastebaskets right over there? *(Points.)*

Millie: Okey doke.

(As the ladies continue to talk, Clara mops and dusts while Millie empties trash baskets, the first into the second, the second into the third. Then she begins dusting and absentmindedly empties trash in reverse order, the third basket into the second, and so on. This emptying and reemptying continue as long as the conversation lasts.)

Millie: Say, Clara, did you hear Mr. Brewster got a new secretary last week? You know him, doncha? He's that handsome young fella that just joined the law office on the fifth floor.

Clara: *(reaching over to Millie)* Pass me that furniture polish, will you?

Millie: Oh, sure. Well, anyway, as I was sayin' about this secretary, they say she's got her eye on him, eligible bachelor that he is an' all, and they say it's just a matter of time a'fore she lands him, with her feminine wiles and all. *(Millie pauses to strike a pose.)* But I don' know, honey. Mark my words, that Mr. Brewster, he's

22

one smart fella. He knows when he's bein' pursued, an' he don't take kindly to it. I *know* he don't. Why I jest know he's the kind o' man as would jest as soon do his own pursuin' and none o' this liberated woman stuff, no ma'am, jest you wait and see. She's gonna find he's gonna give her a run for her money, yes siree! *(Laughs heartily.)* I'm tellin' ya, Clara, that Mr. Brewster, he knows which end is up. There ain't no foolin' him. Why, do you know they say he was tops in his class at Harvard? An' they say he's so smart an' so handsome, an' he knows his law backwards an' for'ards, an'—*(slows down and gropes for words)* an' he's gonna be rich some day, they say, on account o' he's jest the hardest workin' man—an' they all jest love him—an'—an'— an' I know somebody that don't. *I* don't! I *don't!* *(Shakes her fist toward the ceiling and looks up as she does so.)* Do you hear me, Mr. Brewster? They all think yer so smart, but I *don't!* I don't give *that (snaps fingers)* fer yer opinions o' things, Mr. Brewster, so what d'ya think of that? Ain't that jest the berries, Mr. Brewster? Ain't it? *Ain't it?* *(Millie covers her face and begins to sob.)*

Clara: *(Rushes over to her.)* Why, Millie, what is it? You jest ain't yerself tonight! Come on over here an' set a spell an' let's talk. *(Leads her over to a chair, sits down herself, and leaves Millie standing. Millie finds the wastepaper basket with the trash in it, empties the trash on the floor, and turns it upside down. She sits on it beside Clara, still sobbing.)* Now tell me dear, jest what's all this about? What's that beast gone and done to upset you so? There, there. (Clara dries Millie's tears with the hem of her apron.)*

Millie: Oh, Clara! *(Sobs for several seconds.)* Oh, Clara! *(Finally gets hold of herself.)* Oh, Clara, I'm jest so ashamed and humiliated, I kin hardly hold my head up.

Clara: Why, dear, whatever happened? Was you fired?

Millie: Oh no, 'tain't nothin' like that. But if'n things don't change, Mr. Brewster said I jest might be. *(Sobs again.)* You see, it's like this, hon. I was up there cleanin' tonight, an' Mr. Brewster, he was workin' late.

Clara: Yes?

Millie: Well, I walks in an' I sees him, an' I says "Evenin' Mr. Brewster," an' he says "Evenin'," an' then afore I kin even git out another word he starts askin' me questions, one right after another, an' it waren't but a minute an' he was hoppin' mad!

Clara: At you? Whatever for, Millie?

Millie: Well, he started askin' me if I was the one as had cleaned off his desk last night, an' I said yes. An' he asked me did I clean off them papers as was on his desk. An' I said, "What papers was that, Mr. Brewster?" An' he said, "Them papers as was in this little basket here on my desk." An' I sort of brightened right up like an' said, "Yes, sir, Mr. Brewster, I threw them papers right out, jest like it said on the basket, O-U-T." I didn't touch the papers as was in the IN basket, figurin' they was somethin' he'd be needin'. But it was plain to me that he wanted all them papers in the OUT basket out, and so that's where I put 'em. Out. All nice an' tidy. An' Clara, you know what then? He went crazy. *Crazy!* Why, he turned into a wild man before my very eyes an' he screamed somethin' about important papers an' said he was gonna have to work all night an' the next night an' the next, an' he could never replace some of it. An' I kept tellin' him I was sorry, so sorry, but he wouldn't listen. He jest kept screamin' at me, somethin' about "the Sinclair contract!" I picked up my cleanin' stuff and got out of there fast. Last I saw he was sittin' there with his head on his desk, cryin' like a baby. *(Looks forlorn and thoughtful.)*

Clara: You didn't mean no harm, dear. You was jest tryin' to make things neat. *(Pats her shoulder consolingly.)*

Millie: Tell *him* that. Tell me somethin', Clara. Why is it people never appreciate all the right things I do? They never say, "Thanks for the clean floor, Millie." "You done a good job on the windows, Millie." "Sure like the way you dusted, Millie." They never notice the right things I do day in and day out. But boy, they sure notice fast enough when I botch something up.

Clara: Guess it's jest in the nature of folks to be unappreciative. You know, come to think of it, dear, I know somebody who's gone through this sort of thing, somebody who could really understand what you've been going through.

Millie: You do?

Clara: Sure do. This man (*thoughtfully*), well, this man, I guess He was one of a kind.

Millie: What did he do?

Clara: Well, He did jest 'bout most everything, I guess, some preachin', some doctorin'. He even took it upon Himself to feed five thousand people once.

Millie: My, but he must have been a rich man!

Clara: No, He wasn't. As a matter of fact, He didn't even have a home or a bed to sleep in at night. No, He was one of the world's poorest men. But then again, you might say He was the richest.

Millie: Well, what was it he did that folks didn't appreciate?

Clara: Lots of things. Once He healed ten lepers. Only one came back to say thank you.

Millie: My! Ain't that jest the way folks is, though?

Clara: The worst thing came 'bout when He was thirty-three years old, though. He'd been walkin' all over the countryside, teachin', preachin', healin', listenin' to folks, carin' about them. Cried with the ones who hurt, laughed with the ones as was glad. In the end it was the folks He most wanted to help that done Him in.

Millie: Done him *in*? You mean—?

Clara: That's right. They killed Him. Oh, first they had their fun. They stripped Him, whipped Him, spit upon Him, then nailed Him on a cross an' left Him to die.

Millie: Clara, I know who you're talkin' about. It's Jesus, ain't it?

Clara: That's right, Millie. The Bible says, "He was despised."

Millie: (*Gives a low whistle.*) I guess Jesus knew what it means for folks not to appreciate all He done.

Clara: Millie, do *you* appreciate all Jesus done for *you*? I mean, what He done, He done for you and for me. He's offerin' us forgiveness for our sins an' eternity—that's *forever*, Millie!—in heaven with Him, if we jest believe on Him an' trust in Him.

25

Millie: You know, Clara, I don't know if I ever done that. Trust in Jesus, I mean. Do you suppose He feels like I don't appreciate Him? If He done all what you said, seems to me I owe Him somethin'. Appreciation don't really seem like enough.

Clara: It ain't. None of us has got what it takes to pay Jesus back for all He done, but what He wants in return is our lives. Us. He wants us to live for Him, listenin' to Him and doin' it His way, every day. Listen, Millie, we're jest about finished up here. What say you an' me go over to my place for coffee an' we can talk about this more? I think you an' Jesus might like to get to know each other.

Millie: *(smiling)* I'd like that!

(They gather up their equipment and exit, arm in arm.)

Song: "Bring Back the Springtime in My Heart"
Talk: Have a qualified person give a brief talk on having a clean heart, perhaps using Psalm 51:10; 119:9,11; and so on.
Song: "Cleanse Me, O God"
Closing Prayer

5
April

WHAT SHALL WE WEAR?

Style Show: To get your women thinking in the line of *clothing*, start with a style show. Many local dress shops or department stores gladly cooperate by providing garments for your selected models to show. Of course, the models will need to try the clothes on beforehand with the representative from the store.

Bible Reading: Isaiah 64:6; 61:10; 61:3

Prayer

Skit: "What Shall I Wear?"

    Characters: Myrna (wearing a ragged, dirty dress)
                     Rita (wearing a ragged, dirty dress)
                     Messenger Girl (can be dressed in white as an angel)

SCENE I

(Myrna sits in a chair. She hears a knock at the door and goes to answer. A messenger girl enters.)

Messenger: A letter to you from the King!

Myrna: The King? A message to *me* from the King?

Messenger: Yes, Ma'am. *(She hands Myrna a letter and then leaves.)*

Myrna: *(Opens envelope eagerly and reads aloud.)* "You are invited to be a guest at the wedding of My resurrected Son." Oh, how exciting! How wonderful! I must call Rita and tell her! Imagine my getting an invitation like this! Little old me! *(Goes to telephone* *and dials.*) Rita, come on over. I have the most exciting news! (*pause*) No, I don't want to tell you over the phone. I want you to see it with your own eyes. Can you come right away? (*pause*) Good. Hurry! (*Hangs up phone. Walks around the room, looking at the invitation.*) Just imagine! An invitation from the King! A personal invitation to *me*! His Son's wedding! I can't believe it!

(*Rita bursts in.*)

Rita: Well, what is it? I'm dying of curiosity.

(*Myrna hands her the invitation. Rita reads it aloud.*)

Rita: (*Turns the paper over wonderingly.*) This is hard to believe.

Myrna: I know! But isn't it fantastic?

Rita: What are you going to wear?

Myrna: Wear? (*Looks down at her dress.*) I hadn't thought of that.

Rita: You certainly can't wear what you've got on to a wedding. Besides being raggedy, it's filthy!

Myrna: I know. I can't get these spots out. I've tried, but—

Rita: Well, I can't help you. I don't have any clothes to lend you. Sorry about that. Good luck! (*She leaves.*)

Myrna: (*Sinks into a chair.*) A chance of a lifetime, and I don't have anything to wear. Maybe—maybe I can fix this old dress up. I'm going to try. (*Myrna gets needle and thread and starts sewing up a rip on the skirt. It only makes another hole bigger. She sprays something from a can on the stain and rubs hard. Nothing helps. She finally gives up.*) It's no use. I just can't make myself presentable for that wedding. I can't go! After all my efforts, this dress is still a filthy rag. (*She begins to cry. A knock is heard at the door.*)

Myrna: (*Wipes eyes.*) Come in.

Messenger: (*Holds out a large box.*) A gift from the King!

Myrna: For me? (*Takes box and opens it. She lifts out a white garment.*)

Messenger: To wear to the wedding.

Myrna: You mean—

Messenger: The King not only invites you to the wedding of His Son, but also provides suitable clothing to wear.

Myrna: (*wonderingly*) It's beautiful! But I'm afraid I can't afford it. It must cost a lot, and I have no money.

Messenger: This robe will cost you no money; you couldn't possibly pay for it. It cost the King His only Son; it cost the Son His life to provide it for you. It is His righteousness. All you have to do is receive it.

Myrna: Fantastic! I'm most grateful, most grateful!

(Messenger bows and leaves. Myrna tries on the white garment. Rita comes in.)

Rita: Oh, what a beautiful robe—so white and clean! Now you can go to the wedding after all! Where did you get it?

Myrna: From the King Himself!

Rita: How much did it cost?

Myrna: It didn't cost me a dime, but it cost the King's Son His life.

Rita: You didn't even have to *do* anything to get it?

Myrna: I only had to receive it. "I will greatly rejoice in the LORD, my soul will exult in my God; for He has clothed me with garments of salvation. . . . For by grace you have been saved through faith; and that not of yourselves, it is the gift of God" (Isaiah 61:10a; Ephesians 2:8). *(Bows head.)* Thank You, Lord!

Prayer: Ask a woman (having arranged it before the meeting) to lead in a prayer of thanksgiving for the robe of righteousness that Christ has provided for us by His death on the cross. Before she prays, she could invite unsaved women who are in the audience to receive the free gift of salvation Christ offers and thus be clothed in His righteousness.

SCENE II

(Myrna still wears the white robe, but over it she is wearing an apron or a smock of some dull color—it can be made of crepe paper—on which signs are fastened: rainy weather, sink is clogged, baby fussy, children noisy, husband cranky, neighbors nosy, bills piling up, groceries expensive, sinus trouble, gaining weight. Myrna walks about the room so that everyone can read the signs pinned to her apron. She frowns and sighs as if worried and depressed. Rita enters.)

Rita: *(Sits down.)* Hi! You look as though you've lost your best friend.

Myrna: *(Sinks into a chair.)* Not that, but everything else is going wrong. I wish I'd never gotten up this morning.

Rita: It's not as great as you thought it would be, is it?

Myrna: What's not as great?

Rita: Being a Christian. You were so excited and happy at first that I really envied you, but I see it didn't last. Nothing good ever does.

Myrna: *(Frowns thoughtfully.)* I hate to hear you talk like that, Rita. I still have my robe of righteousness. *(Lifts up apron.)* See? That means my sins are forgiven and I'm on my way to the King's wedding feast in heaven some day.

Rita: But you don't seem very happy about it anymore. All you ever do is grumble. As I said, being a Christian isn't all that great. Heaven is a long way off—doesn't help you any now with your sinus trouble and family problems. *(Yawns.)* Wish I could help you, but I've got troubles of my own. Got to go now. Come on over if you want a shoulder to cry on. *(Rita leaves.)*

Myrna: *(Stands up.)* I really blew it! Rita was interested in becoming a Christian, but now she's changed her mind. And my complaining did it. *(Clasps hands and looks up.)* Lord, forgive me. I'm really glad You saved me, but I get so bogged down with all my problems. Maybe if I read my Bible—*(Myrna sits down and opens her Bible. Someone knocks on the door.)* Come in.

Messenger: *(Holds out a box.)* Here is another gift from the King.

Myrna: *(wonderingly as she takes the box)* Whatever can it be! *(Takes out a white cape with signs pinned on it: "All things work together for good"; "I will never leave you"; "The Lord is good"; "The Lord is my strength"; "I shall not want"; "He giveth more grace"; "My grace is sufficient.")* What is this?

Messenger: A garment of praise. The King invites you to wear it instead of the one you have on. You can make an exchange if you want to. *(Pauses.)* Do you want it?

Myrna: You mean, I have a choice?

Messenger: *(Nods.)* Lots of Christians refuse to wear it. They prefer their complaining and self-pity.

Myrna: *(Looks down at her apron, hesitates, then tears it off and hands it to the messenger.)* Yes, I'll make the exchange. *(She puts on the cape.)* All these wonderful promises! How can I be glum? How can I help but praise! I feel better already.

Messenger: The King suggests you put it on even when you don't *feel* like it. The garment of praise is guaranteed to lift your spirits if you give it a chance. It glorifies the King, too.

Myrna: I will! I'll wear it every day. I can't wait to show Rita. Maybe this will convince her to become a Christian. Please tell the King I am most grateful.

(Messenger bows and leaves, taking the apron with her. Myrna smooths the garment lovingly.)

Myrna: The garment of praise! How beautiful! Lord, forgive me for not praising before. When I stop to think, there are dozens of reasons to praise You. Thank You, Lord. Thank You very much. You give "beauty for ashes, the oil of joy for mourning, the garment of praise for the spirit of heaviness" (Isaiah 61:3, KJV). *

Song: "Praise Him, Praise Him" or "Jesus, I Just Want to Thank You"

Testimonies: Have several women (having arranged this before the meeting) tell how God worked through their praises, how they overcame grumbling, self-pity, and other, similar faults.

YOU SAID IT! (A PUPPET PROGRAM)

Make three hand puppets. Paper sacks will do, but cloth ones would be better. Make two women, Minnie and Dora. Be sure to put bright colors on their faces so they will show up. Make each with a different color of yarn hair to tell them apart. For the third puppet, make a tongue. Color or paint it red. If it doesn't look authentic, write "tongue" on it.

---

*King James Version.

An elaborate stage is not necessary to put on this puppet show. One can be made from a refrigerator or stove carton, as pictured. If that does not seem feasible, simply use a screen, a piano, or a folding table on its side with the top toward the audience; or string a wire across the room and hang a curtain or sheet on it.

PROGRAM

Introduction: (*This can be given by a puppet if you have an extra one, or by your program chairman.*) During this puppet show, it is very easy to think of the person next to you or in the row ahead of you. Or your thoughts may fly to your mother-in-law. *If only she could hear this!* you might think. Please apply the truths of our puppet show to yourself, not to anyone else. Promise? I knew you would.

(*Minnie and Tongue appear.*)

Tongue: You look sad. May I ask what's wrong?

Minnie: Oh, I don't know. I just feel so—so unwanted. My friends are ignoring me. Even my husband doesn't seem to want to be around me anymore.

Tongue: Can you think of a reason for this?

Minnie: It's not my fault. I try. I—why am I telling you this? Who are you, anyway?

32

Tongue: I'm your tongue.

Minnie: My tongue!

(Tongue nods.)

Tongue: Don't look down on me. I may be small, but I'm powerful. As the Good Book says: "Life and death are in the power of the tongue."

Minnie: Life and death? You mean you can kill people?

Tongue: *(Nods.)* Not physically, but in other ways. I can kill people's enthusiasm, their hopes; I can cut down their self-esteem, discourage them to the point where they'll give up. I can harm people spiritually and ruin their reputations.

Minnie: You—you wouldn't!

Tongue: I can do just the opposite, too—bring life.

Minnie: For instance—

Tongue: I can lift up people who are down, encourage them to try again, make them feel wanted, boost their self-esteem, build them up, tell them about the Lord.

Minnie: Fantastic!

Tongue: On the other hand, I can pierce and wound.

Minnie: How dreadful! What do you use to perform such deeds?

Tongue: Cruel words.

Minnie: *(slowly)* Cruel words?

Tongue: *(Nods.)* Sometimes they are simply thoughtless, careless words, but they wound feelings, deflate egos, and destroy self-confidence.

Minnie: Does gossip come under that category?

Tongue: Yes, indeed. Gossip is one of the best spears I have. It can separate friends, bring heartache, ruin reputations. The Bible says: "The words of a talebearer are as wounds" (Proverbs 18:8, KJV).

Minnie: I can't imagine a little thing like you doing all that!

Tongue: Sure I'm little, but don't underestimate my power. As the Good Book says, "The tongue is a small part of the body, and yet it boasts of great things. Behold, how great a forest is set aflame by such a small fire!" (James 3:5).

Minnie: Just imagine the damage—

Tongue: The Bible also says, "But no one can tame the tongue; it is a restless evil and full of deadly poison. With it we bless our Lord and Father; and with it we curse men, who have been made in the likeness of God" (James 3:8-9).

Minnie: *(Hangs head.)* Blessing and cursing? Poison? Yes, just this morning! I didn't really mean those nasty words I said to my husband. And when Johnny spilled his milk for the third morning in a row—

Tongue: "There is one who speaks rashly like the thrusts of a sword, but the tongue of the wise brings healing" (Proverbs 12:18).

Minnie: So you can do something good, too.

Tongue: Yes, indeed. I can heal wounds. As I said before, I can lift spirits, boost self-esteem, encourage.

(Dora pops up.)

Dora: May I say something? I've been listening to your conversation. I have a problem. At least my husband thinks I have. He says I talk too much.

Tongue: "A fool's voice is known by multitude of words" (Ecclesiastes 5:3, KJV).

Dora *(to Minnie)***:** He doesn't mean me, does he? I know I talk a lot, but I'm nervous, and all nervous people do. *(Talks faster.)* My mother was like that and my grandmother, all nervous and all talkers. And on my father's side there were Aunt Lena and Aunt Henrietta. They were good women and all, but try to shut them up—

Tongue: *(Interrupts.)* "Even a fool, when he keeps silent, is considered wise" (Proverbs 17:28a).

Dora: Oh, I think he does mean me. I'm getting out of here. *(Dora leaves.)*

Minnie: I'm glad that chatterbox left. Now I can talk to you about my tongue trouble. That's why I'm so miserable—I've been hurting people with my tongue, and now they're all shunning me. I wonder why God gave me a tongue when it does so much mischief?

Tongue: He never intended that it should. Under His control, I become a great power for good.

Minnie: The healing bit, you mean, bolstering people's spirits, saying a good word.

Tongue: Yes, and praising God. The psalmist said: "My mouth is filled with Thy praise. . . . My tongue also will utter Thy righteousness all day long" (Psalm 71:8a, 24a).

Minnie: Praise God all day long? I'm not sure—

Tongue: (*Interrupts.*) Most people would rather grumble.

Minnie: You mean, we have a choice?

Tongue: Right. You can yield your tongue to the Lord and let Him help you control it, or you can stubbornly say like the people in David's day: "With our tongue we will prevail; our lips are our own; who is lord over us?" (Psalm 12:4).

(*Dora reappears.*)

Dora: (*breathlessly*) I'm back. I found a passage in the Bible about the tongue. Bet you don't know this one. I was looking through my Bible, feeling bad about being so talkative—you know it runs in the family. My mother and grandmother, Aunt Lena and Aunt Henrietta, not to mention—

Tongue: (*interrupting*) Don't mention it then. Tell us the verse.

Dora: "A gentle answer turns away wrath, but a harsh word stirs up anger. . . . A soothing tongue is a tree of life" (Proverbs 15:1, 4a). I didn't find that one about talking too much. Are you sure it's in the Bible?

Minnie: (*impatiently*) Of course it is, Dora! Would you mind being quiet? Oh, I'm sorry. I didn't mean to hurt you. I should build you up instead. I like your outfit, and—let's see—you're very good with words.

Dora: Thank you. That's the nicest thing anyone has said to me all day.

(*Tongue disappears.*)

Minnie: I'm going to practice saying nice things from now on— soothing words instead of sharp ones. I'm going to try to heal instead of hurt. I'm asking the Holy Spirit to help me control my tongue and use it for good instead of evil, and for praising God, too.

Dora: And I'm asking Him to help me not talk so much. Did I ever tell you about the time Aunt Henrietta went to the dentist and he filled her mouth with instruments and she couldn't talk and it was so hard on her she had a stroke and—

Minnie: *(looking around and interrupting)* Where is Tongue?

Dora: Out doing some mischief, do you suppose? Throwing spears, wounding people, cutting them down, ruining their reputations by gossiping?

Minnie: I don't think so.

Dora: Why not?

Minnie: Because he can't do that all by himself. He can't do any of those things unless we let him.

Dora: I never thought of that. *(Pauses.)* Then the responsibility rests with us!

Minnie: Come on, Dora, let's have a little prayer meeting and ask the Lord to help us control our tongues and use them for His glory.

Dora: *(as they disappear off stage)* Sure. If only Aunt Henrietta had done this, she probably wouldn't have had that stroke!

6
May

CELEBRATE CHILDHOOD

Children's Day in Japan is May 5. Does your meeting time fall near that date? If so, you may choose to focus on one of the following themes:

1. Your mission work in Japan
2. Christian Home Week, with emphasis on family relationships or biblical discipline of children.
3. Children's Homes (if your church sponsors them)
4. Child Evangelism (if you sponsor such programs)

SUGGESTED PROGRAM OUTLINE

Scripture Reading: Matthew 19:13-14 (*while group stands*)
Special Music: A children's choir
Program
Testimony and Prayer Time: (*Ask for prayer requests.*)

PROGRAM CONTENT SUGGESTIONS (CHOOSE ONE ONLY)

1. *Japan:* Have the women remove their shoes at the door. Sit on cushions around low tables (borrowed from the children's Sunday school classes). Serve tea from pretty cups. Display curios, costumes, and maps from Japan.

Program leader, wear kimono if possible. Bow low from the waist, with hands low on your thighs and say "Konnichi Wa" ("Good Day") or "Komban Wa" ("Good Evening").

Program Leader: Festivals and children are very important in Japan. There is a festival somewhere in Japan almost every day of the year. Children enjoy all of them. There are special ones just for them. During World War II, the Japanese government decided to have one big celebration for children. It combined Boys' Day and Girls' Day into a holiday called Children's Day. This is held on May 5, the original date for Boys' Day. (March 3 was Girls' Day.)

Many Japanese still celebrate both the original holidays, however. On March 3, girls display all the ceremonial dolls in the home, and on May 5, boys display their collections of warrior dolls. The family also flies a multicolored paper carp (fish kite) from a bamboo pole for each son in the family. The kites symbolize the hope that the sons will be brave like the courageous carp fish. During those special times for the children, relatives and friends visit and eat special food together.

Give the women information, letters, and pictures of your missionaries to Japan. Teach the chorus only of "Jesus Loves Me" in Japanese to the women or some children. Sing it as a closing prayer.

"Jesus Loves Me"

(Pronunciation: a, e—short vowel sound; o—long vowel sound; i— long "e" sound; u—"oo" sound as in moo; ai—"ah-ee" sound)

Wa ga Shu E-su
Wa ga Shu E-su
Wa ga Shu E-su
Wa-re wo ai-i-su.

2. *Christian Home Week:* Read and discuss Ephesians 5:15—6:4 and Colossians 3:12-21.

3. *Children's Homes:* Hear a progress report on the home you sponsor. Plan or do a service project for them.

4. *Child Evangelism:* Invite a teacher of a Good News Club to pretend you are children and lead you in a typical club meeting. Have a question and answer time, and offer an opportunity for women to volunteer to teach or host a club in their homes.

The above three programs not chosen at this time could be used some other time when you need a special feature.

BLOOM WHERE YOU'RE PLANTED
(A MOTHER-DAUGHTER TEA)

Decorate the tables with African violets in bloom, if possible.

PROGRAM

Song: "M Is for the Million Things You Gave Me"
(You can find this classic at a music store; add this second verse to the daughters.)

    D is for the dirty knees and scratches,
    A means you're an angel when asleep;
    U means you're unique; there's no one like you,
    G means you're a girl so dear and sweet.
    H stands for the hugs and
    T imes we treasure,
    E is every
    R eason you're so dear.

    Put them all together, they spell DAUGHTER, the word that means the world to me!

Song: "Tall and Short" Tune: "Reuben and Rachel"

From: *Voices of America* (Together We Sing Series) Wolfe, Krone, Fullerton. Editor-Max T. Krone, Follett Publishing Co., Chicago.

Tall (All those over 5'4" tall sing.)

We are long and tall and skinny, lank and thin we will admit;
But our appetite is perfect, and we're always feeling fit.

Short (All those under 5'4" sing.)

We are short and stout and rugged, and our stature may be wide;
But with it we are contented, we accept our size with pride.

Tall

We would not be like some people, short, condensed—a sorry plight;
With spike heels and high poke bonnets, helping elevate their height.

Short

We are not a bit peculiar; we are chic and so petite;
No one ever could mistake us for a lamppost on the street.

All

Short and tall we should be thinking, I'll help you and you help me;
If we plan and work together, How successful we will be!

Solo: "I'm Something Special," to be sung by a young girl

Skit: "Bloom Where You're Planted" by Judy Erickson, Evie Haglund, and Karen Bakken

Characters: Shrinking Violet No. 1
Shrinking Violet No. 2
Daisy Mae
Rose Red
Gardener (with fertilizer)
Lady (owner of the garden)

(Dress up each flower to look like its name. Use art tissue to make blossoms to frame the face. The violets are standing in the garden. Daisy Mae comes skipping in, acting "fresh as a daisy." Violets look at her, then at each other, and sigh.)

Violet No. 1: Look at that new spring outfit. She always looks so perky!

Violet No. 2: I wish I had yellow petals instead of purple.

40

Violet No. 1: Yes, and I wish I could take the sun as well as she does. All I do is burn.

(Rose Red enters like a regal beauty queen.)

Violet No. 1: I wish I knew what fragrance she's wearing.

Violet No. 2: Yes, all we ever smell like is bug dust. Some gardener we've got! Whoever put us in this corner sure didn't know what he was doing!

Violet No. 1: That's for sure. I need good, rich soil, and all that's here for me is clay. I'll never bloom here. *(Starts to cry.)*

Violet No. 2: There are so many weeds around us—nobody notices us. We're not good enough for anyone's bouquet.

(Both cry and blow noses.)

Violet No. 1: Did you hear that Chrysanthemum got picked for someone's centerpiece? And Baby's Breath will be used at a wedding.

Violet No. 2: Yes, and not only that, but the Carnation sisters get picked for everything. It's enough to make you wilt! Sh, here comes the gardener. Let's see who she picks this time.

(Gardener walks in, sets down a box labeled "Fertilizer," and walks off.)

Violet No. 2: *(Gives other violet the elbow.)* Here's our chance! You should see what it does for the Petunias! Here, I'll sprinkle some on you, and you sprinkle some on me. *(Pretends to sprinkle on fertilizer.)* Ooh! I feel better already.

Violet No. 1: Feels so good! Put on some more!

Red Rose: *(Shakes head.)* You'd better not do that.

Violet No. 1: *(defensively)* Who are you to advise! You've never been left lonely and neglected because nobody noticed you. *(Heaps on more fertilizer.)*

Rose Red: *(Shakes head and walks off.)* You'll be sorry. You were better off before.

Violet No. 1: Ooh, I think I'm beginning to burn. *(Looks at her leaves.)* I have such tender skin.

Violet No. 2: I think I'm getting sick. I don't think this was such a good idea. Maybe Rose Red was right!

(Violets stand quietly, drooping. Lady enters with watering can.)

Lady: Oh, what's happened to my beautiful violets? The gardener must have put too much fertilizer on them by mistake. I do hope they're not going to die. I'd hoped to use them for the Mother-Daughter Tea!

(Violets look at each other big-eyed. Lady puts down her things, scrapes away the fertilizer, fusses over them, and waters them.)

Lady: I think they'll be all right by Tuesday. *(Walks off.)*

Violets: *(Join stems, dance around, and speak in unison.)* Did you hear that? We'll be used at the Mother-Daughter Tea!

Violet No. 1: I guess the gardener who put us here knew what he was doing after all!

Violet No. 2: Yes. I guess *we'll bloom where we're planted!*

Talk: "Bloom—Who, Me?"

Bloom where I'm planted? Who, me? But you don't know my circumstances!

The Bible abounds with illustrations of people who bloomed even in extremely difficult situations. Joseph was cruelly torn from his family and planted in far-off Egypt when only a teenager. There he was sold as a slave to Potiphar. He could have become resentful at that turn of events. Instead, he bloomed where he was planted. Because of that, Potiphar made him the overseer of his entire household.

Suddenly disaster struck again. Potiphar's wife tried to seduce Joseph. When he refused, she accused him to her husband of the very thing he had refused to do. As a result, he was thrown into prison. Joseph again could have become bitter; instead, he bloomed where he was planted. Soon the jailer made him his right-hand man in prison.

One day when two of the prisoners looked sad, Joseph, who was blooming where he was planted, asked them the reason for their sadness. The two prisoners told Joseph about strange dreams they'd had that they couldn't understand. Joseph interpreted the dreams for them. One of the prisoners was killed and the other released, but Joseph was left in prison for two more long years, two more years of blooming where he was planted.

Finally Joseph was released from prison to interpret a dream for the Pharoah. He was so impressed with Joseph that he made him the second ruler in the land. God then used Joseph to devise a plan whereby the Egyptians and other peoples, including Joseph's own family, were saved from starvation during years of famine. He was still blooming where he was planted.

Joseph would never have reached his high position had he not bloomed also when he was planted as a slave in Potiphar's house and as a prisoner in the Egyptian dungeon.

Perhaps your circumstances are not so pleasant, either. You look back and say, "If only!" You look forward and say, "What if?" God wants you to leave both the past and the future with Him. He wants you to make the most of right now—today. He wants you to bloom where He has planted you.

Because Joseph bloomed when he was in unpleasant and difficult circumstances, God made him a ruler of Egypt with great power and influence. He has also promised us glory if we will be faithful where He has planted us. Paul said: "For momentary, light affliction is producing for us an eternal weight of glory far beyond all comparison" (2 Corinthians 4:17).

It is easier to bloom where we're planted when we realize that God has planted us where we are. He has a plan and purpose for even His seemingly most insignificant plants. So let's bloom where He has placed us; yes, right where we are!

Variation on Talk: "My Mother Bloomed Where She Was Planted"

If one of your members has an unusual mother or grandmother, she may want to give a talk about her, telling how she bloomed where she was planted, made the best of her circumstances, and became a blessing to her children and others.

7

June

PUZZLE OR PLAN

Leader: (*Start with the riddle below. See if your ladies can guess it by the first clue. If not, go on to the others.*)

First Clue: The farther I go, the shorter my tail, and I come home without it.

Second Clue: A little pony; every jump he stops a gap.

Third Clue: A little naked thing that clothes others.

Fourth Clue: A slender fellow with one leg and one eye.

Answer: A needle

Sometimes life is like a riddle. We can't find the answer. "Why is this happening to me?" we ask. This evening we will discover that the characters of the Bible were also puzzled about the events in their lives. Let's learn from their experiences.

Song: "All the Way My Savior Leads Me"

Prayer

Interview:

Characters Needed:

Interviewer

Job's Wife, Naomi, Esther (*Pin name on each. If possible, have them dressed in long dresses and shawls. Naomi's dress should be plain, but those of the other two can be quite ornate.*)

Interviewer: This is station W-O-R-D. Tonight we are going to discuss the topic "Puzzle or Plan." Let's interview some people from the past. Mrs. Job, your husband is famous for what he went

44

through. Come to think of it, you went through quite a bit yourself. Would you like to tell us about it?

Mrs. Job: Well, we lost everything. First our oxen and donkeys, then our sheep and camels, and finally our ten children. Everything was wiped out.

Interviewer: Were you puzzled about this turn of events?

Job's Wife: That's putting it mildly.

Interviewer: We read in the Bible that your husband, Job, worshiped God and said, "Naked I came from my mother's womb, and naked I shall return there. . . . Blessed be the name of the LORD" (Job 1:21). Was that your response, too?

Mrs. Job: No! I was angry with God. When He let my husband become afflicted with boils on top of everything else, I told my husband to curse God and die.

Interviewer: Did you think God might have a plan in allowing all of this?

Mrs. Job: No, I thought He was cruel.

Interviewer: Let's interview someone else here from the past. Naomi, as I remember from the Bible, you had a rather hard time as well.

Naomi: Yes. My husband and I moved from Judah to Moab with our two sons because there was famine in Judah. Our sons grew up and married girls of Moab, but then disaster struck.

Interviewer: Your husband died?

Naomi: Not only my husband, but my two sons as well.

Interviewer: That must have been very hard to go through.

Naomi: It was devastating. I complained against the Lord for His dealings with me. When I returned to my own country with Ruth, my daughter-in-law, I told my friends not to call me Naomi anymore, because that means "Pleasant." I asked them to call me Mara, meaning "Bitter."

Interviewer: You were bitter?

Naomi: Yes, I'm afraid so.

Interviewer: You believed that God was responsible for all your misfortune?

Naomi: He is over all. He permits whatever happens to us.

Interviewer: How true! Well, let's see what this young lady has to say. Esther, I understand you didn't have such an easy life either.

Esther: No, I was brought up in captivity in Persia. My father and mother died when I was small, so my cousin Mordecai brought me up.

Interviewer: I'm sure it wasn't easy to be a captive in a land that wasn't your own.

Esther: It certainly wasn't. We never felt secure. We were exiles from the land of Israel, and our captors never let us forget it. Some of them despised us Jews.

Interviewer: Can you think of an especially traumatic experience you went through?

Esther: The most traumatic time of my life was when I was taken to the king's palace to "try out" for queen. I didn't want to be the wife of a heathen monarch. But to not be chosen as his wife would have been even worse; I would have had to spend the rest of my life as one of his many concubines.

Interviewer: But you were chosen.

Esther: Yes, God arranged that.

Interviewer: It must not have been an easy life, being the queen of King Ahasuerus. He had a practice of putting to death anyone who came into his presence without an invitation. Right?

Esther: Right. Unless he was in a good mood and held out his golden scepter.

Interviewer: Not exactly a comfortable relationship. Before I ask you anything more, let's ask these other ladies a few questions. Mrs. Job, can you tell us how your great trial turned out?

Mrs. Job: It had a happy ending in spite of my anger against God. My husband wasn't angry, only bewildered. He kept trusting God. Finally God healed him of his boils and gave him twice as much as he had had before in the way of possessions. He even gave us ten more children.

Interviewer: Fantastic! Can you see any reason why God put you and your husband through all that?

Job's Wife: Actually, we found out later it was Satan's idea. He thought Job was serving God just for what he could get. God permitted Satan to test Job to show that wasn't true.

Interviewer: And he came through the test with flying colors. Job has been an example of patience to sufferers down through the years. Would you say there was a plan in this puzzle, that Romans 8:28 was true in your case—"God causes all things to work together for good to those who love God"?

Job's Wife: Yes, I'll have to admit that.

Interviewer: Naomi, did anything good come out of your hardships?

Naomi: Oh, yes! We were so poor when we returned to my own country of Judah that my daughter-in-law Ruth had to glean after the reapers in the barley fields in order for us to get food. God led her to the field of a relative of my husband's, named Boaz. This godly, wealthy man eventually became Ruth's husband.

Interviewer: And you?

Naomi: I became a member of their household and had no more financial worries. I also became a happy grandmother!

Interviewer: So you allowed your friends to call you Naomi again?

Naomi: Yes, of course! It was a mistake to feel bitter toward God and complain. If I had only known the pleasant surprises He had in store for me!

Interviewer: God says through Jeremiah: "I know the plans that I have for you . . . plans for welfare and not for calamity to give you a future and a hope" (Jeremiah 29:11).

Naomi: Exactly! He had a wonderful plan for me, but I was too discouraged to see it. True to His promise, however, He gave me a future and a hope.

Interviewer: Esther, your story had a happy ending, too, I hear.

Esther: It seemed anything but happy for a while when Haman was working to destroy my people.

Interviewer: And Mordecai asked you to go in to see the king without being invited! You could have been killed!

Esther: I realized God had placed me in the palace for this purpose—to save my people. We put the matter in God's hands.

And the king not only accepted me, but he also put Haman to death and reversed his decree against the Jews.

Interviewer: There was a plan in the puzzle, then?

Esther: Yes, a glorious plan.

Interviewer: Through what you ladies are saying, I see that God works out something beautiful even through the plans of Satan and wicked men. As it is written in the Old Testament, "He turned the curse into a blessing." That is very encouraging to us modern Christians. We have trials, too, perhaps not as spectacular as yours, but very real, nonetheless. From your testimonies, we realize anew that God works all things together for good to those who love God. In view of that, it would seem that we should praise Him at the beginning of our trials instead of waiting until the end. That would show our confidence in His love and wisdom. Let's read some verses about this from Scripture.

Scripture Reading: (*Arrange for Scripture readers from the audience before the meeting.*) Psalm 34:1; Ephesians 5:20; 1 Thessalonians 5:18

Interviewer: Perhaps someone in our audience would like to tell us about your experience of how God worked through a trial and brought something good out of it in your life.

Testimony Time

Songs: "Through It All" and "I Know Who Holds the Future"

WHAT A SONG CAN DO! (HYMN PROGRAM)

*The histories of a number of hymns are discussed in this program. If going all the way through would take too long for your meeting, choose your favorite stories to make a program of suitable length. Use a number of different readers. *

Reader: A young man was walking the streets of Ketchikan, Alaska, deeply discouraged. He had become a Christian a short time before, but now, far from home and without Christian fellowship, we was ready to give up. How could he continue living for God when everyone around him was going in the opposite direction?

Suddenly a song came to the young man's mind and lips. To his amazement, he began to hum the words of George Matheson's immortal hymn, "O Love That Will Not Let Me Go." The young man took courage as he realized that he was not alone after all—God was there, holding, strengthening, loving, and keeping him.

Reader: Mr. J. C. Penney was in the hospital. The economic crash of 1929 had left him financially ruined and broken in health. Extremely depressed and without hope, he thought only of death. One morning he felt compelled to leave his hospital room. As he walked down the hall, he came upon a group of people singing the hymn, "God Will Take Care of You." The words of the song gave him new courage. All was not lost—God was still caring for him. And with returning hope came returning health. Mr. Penney was able to rise above his losses and again become a successful businessman.

Reader: During the Civil War, a young Union soldier was assigned to guard duty one dark night. He felt depressed as he shouldered his gun and went to his post, knowing the danger he was in. As he paced back and forth, he thought of his home, his family, and his God. He began to sing the familiar strains of the well-loved hymn "Jesus, Lover of My Soul." An enemy soldier crept near with his rifle. Coming closer, he lifted it to his shoulder and aimed. Just then the Union soldier sang:

> "Cover my defenseless head
> With the shadow of thy wing."

---

*These hymn stories are from the following books:
1. Clint Bonner, *A Hymn is Born* (Chicago: Wilcox and Follet, 1952), pp. 2,3,20,26,94.
2. F. W. Boreham, *A Bunch of Everlastings* (Philadelphia: Judson, 1920), pp. 224-33.
3. Ernest K. Emurian, *Hymn Stories for Programs* (Grand Rapids: Baker, 1963), pp. 37,38,64-66.
4. Cecil Northcott, *Hymns We Love* (Philadelphia: Westminster, 1954), p. 129.

The Confederate soldier dropped his gun, unable to shoot. Years after the war was over, the two men met and reminisced about that memorable night and the song that had saved the soldier's life.

Throughout history, God has used hymns and gospel songs to sustain, encourage, protect, inspire, and even save the lives of His children. Perhaps you have an experience of your own with a gospel song that you would like to tell us about at the end of the program.

How did those wonderful hymns and gospel songs come to be written? Listen, and we will tell you.

Reader: In the early history of the church, it was considered sinful to sing words in a church service except those taken directly from the Bible. The congregational singing, if there was any, consisted of psalms chanted or sung.

In 1674, a homely, scrawny boy was born in England. His name was Isaac Watts. Although he was far from handsome, he had a brilliant mind. He read unceasingly and was so delighted with poetry that he began to speak in rhyme. That irritated his father, who threatened to beat him if he did not stop rhyming. Isaac cried out with tears:

> "Oh father, do some pity take
> And I will no more verses make."

One day when Isaac Watts was fifteen, he came home from a church service disgusted with the poor music used in worship.

"Give us something better, young man," retorted his father.

Isaac immediately set to work writing hymns for the church. He is called "The Father of English Hymnody" because he was the first to bring hymns of nonbiblical composition into the church and establish congregational singing.

Isaac Watts wrote many hymns. One of the best-known is "When I Survey the Wondrous Cross."

Hymn: "When I Survey the Wondrous Cross" (*Sing one or two verses as a congregation.*)

Reader: John Newton's mother died when he was seven. His father sent him to a boarding school where the master was extremely harsh. John left school at the age of ten and went to sea with his father when he was only eleven. Although he often thought of his mother's Christian teaching and tried to be good, more often he yielded to his baser impulses and lived like the rough seamen with whom he associated. By the time he was eighteen, he was a hardened sinner with no use for God and was often in trouble with his superiors. To get away from the captain of the ship he was working on and to abandon himself to sinful living, he hired himself out to a slave trader in Africa. His new master's black wife made life miserable for him, and he was degraded to being a slave of slaves.

After a number of years in this sorry condition, his father arranged his rescue. He was bound for England when a terrific storm threatened to wreck the ship on which he was sailing. As he faced almost certain death, he cried to God for mercy. He could hardly believe that God would extend mercy to him who had blasphemed His name and even tried to persuade others to do so, but as he read the Bible he became assured of God's forgiveness through Christ. Miraculously, the ship made it through the storm and limped into port several months later.

John Newton later gave up the sea to become a preacher of the gospel, as well as a writer of hymns. When he considered what God had saved him from, his gratitude broke out into verse, resulting in the popular hymn "Amazing Grace."

Hymn: "Amazing Grace" *(Sing one or two verses as a congregation.)*
Reader: One of John Newton's contemporaries was William Cowper, who helped him in his ministry and with him compiled a book of hymns called *The Olney Hymns.*

William Cowper was extremely sensitive. Having lost his mother at an early age, he was sent to a boarding school where no one understood him. He received such rough treatment at school that he could not recall it later without a shudder.

Although he studied law and wrote beautiful poetry, he was afflicted with fits of deep depression and insanity, at which times he attempted suicide. The reason for his depression was the guilt of his sin. If only he could find forgiveness and cleansing!

One morning when he was a patient at a Dr. Cotton's private lunatic asylum, he awoke feeling more cheerful than usual.

51

Reaching for the Bible he had thrown aside, he began to search for comfort from its pages. His eyes fell on Romans 3:24-25: "Being justified freely by his grace through the redemption that is in Christ Jesus: whom God hath set forth to be a propitiation through faith in his blood, to declare his righteousness" (KJV).

"Immediately I received strength to believe," said Cowper, "and the full beams of the Sun of Righteousness shone upon me. I saw the sufficiency of the atonement He had made, my pardon in His blood, and the fullness and completeness of His justification. In a moment I believed and received the Gospel."

At last William Cowper had found relief from his burden of sin. Surely it was that experience that led him to write the beautiful hymn "There Is a Fountain Filled with Blood."

Hymn: "There Is a Fountain" (*Sing one or two verses as a congregation.*)

Reader: Porridge for breakfast! Potatoes for lunch! Potatoes for supper! Day after day it was the same menu for the Reverend John Fawcett and his family. The parishioners at Wainsgate would have liked to provide more for their pastor, but they were extremely poor themselves. Although they had erected a crude church in which to hold services, they could not afford to pay their preacher an adequate salary.

John Fawcett was accustomed to poverty. Orphaned at the age of 12, he had been apprenticed to a tailor, which was little better than slavery in those days. He worked for his master from six in the morning until eight at night. Then, when he should have been sleeping, he was reading *Pilgrim's Progress* in his little attic room by the light of a flickering candle. The reading of *Pilgrim's Progress*, together with a sermon he heard from George Whitefield, brought the orphan boy to Christ. He felt called to be a minister.

After many struggles, he was finally ordained and sent to Wainsgate, which was not really a town but a group of straggling houses on a barren hill. In spite of the people's poverty, however, the work flourished and people were brought to Christ. How the people loved their pastor!

One day John Fawcett received a call from a church in London. They offered him a bigger salary, a wider field of service, and a chance for self-improvement. John and his wife, Mary, accepted the call.

As they packed their belongings in a two-wheeled cart, their parishioners crowded around to mourn their going. Many wept as they said good-bye to their beloved pastor and his wife. Then, suddenly, John Fawcett stopped putting things in the wagon.

"We can't go and leave these people," he said to his wife. She agreed. They began unloading the wagon as the people cheered. That night Mr. Fawcett wrote the words to "Blest Be the Tie That Binds," and the next morning he introduced it to his congregation, preaching from Luke 12:15: "A man's life consisteth not in the abundance of the things which he possesseth" (KJV).

John Fawcett stayed in Wainsgate many more years. God honored his self-sacrifice and gave him a ministry of writing as well as preaching. He became famous for his literary work.

Hymn: "Blest Be the Tie That Binds" (*Sing one or two verses as a congregation.*)

Reader: Many a great hymn has been born in a broken heart and written through scalding tears. Consider George Matheson, engaged to be married when he was stricken with blindness. His fiancée broke the engagement. Brokenhearted, Mr. Matheson turned to Christ for comfort. Later he wrote the beautiful song "O Love That Will Not Let Me Go."

Hymn: "O Love That Will Not Let Me Go" (*Sing one or two verses as a congregation.*)

Reader: Andre Crouch, popular contemporary singer and songwriter, in the story of his life, *Through It All,* tells how he wrote the song with that same title when he lost the girl he loved.

Song: "Through It All" (*Sing one or two verses as a congregation.*)

Reader: Elisha Hoffman was no stranger to sorrow. He wrote the chorus of "Leaning on the Everlasting Arms" to comfort two friends who had each lost his wife within days of the other. Mr. Hoffman lost his own wife when she was only thirty-two. One day when making pastoral calls, he came upon a sorrowing woman. Wringing her hands in despair, she cried, "Brother Hoffman, what shall I do? What shall I do?" The sympathetic pastor, after quoting a passage of Scripture, said to her, "You cannot do better than take all your sorrows to Jesus. You must tell Jesus."

"Yes, I must tell Jesus," responded the woman. She proceeded to do so and was immensely comforted.

After that experience, Mr. Hoffman went directly home and wrote the lines of this song that has encouraged brokenhearted people throughout the world to take their cares and problems to Jesus.

Hymn: "I Must Tell Jesus" (*Sing one or two verses as a congregation.*)

Reader: Charles Weigle had his own personal heartbreak when his wife left him "for the bright lights," as she put it, taking their precious little daughter with her. Only God's comfort prevented the distraught man from throwing himself into the Biscayne Bay to end his life. From that experience came the gospel hymn "No One Ever Cared for Me Like Jesus."

Hymn: "No One Ever Cared for Me Like Jesus" (*Sing one or two verses as a congregation.*)

Reader: Mr. Stafford had lost all his personal possessions in the great Chicago fire, but he was grateful that his family had escaped the inferno. He sent his wife and four children to France on a luxury liner, the "Ville du Havre," preparing to join them in a few days. Several days out to sea, however, the liner was rammed by an English sailing vessel and sank. Mr. Stafford's four children went down with the ship.

The stricken man boarded a ship at once to go to his grieving wife. As the ship he sailed on passed by the approximate place where his children had drowned, Mr. Stafford tossed restlessly on his bunk. But God came to him and gave him a song, "It Is Well with My Soul." God comforted the sorrowing man with those words even as He has used the song since that time to comfort countless others. As we sing it together, think of how God is with you also in the hard places of your life.

Hymn: "It Is Well with My Soul" (*Sing one or two verses as a congregation.*)

Reader: Lelia Naylor Morris walked to the altar three different times in an effort to be saved until a man came and laid his hand on her head, saying: "Why, little girl, God is here and ready to forgive your sins." That settled it!

Lelia was musical from the time she was small. She learned to play the piano even though she kept busy helping her widowed mother provide for the family. At the age of thirty, after she had married, she discovered that God had given her a gift for songwriting. Lelia Morris's most well-known hymn is "Nearer, Still Nearer."

(*Read verses.*)

> Nearer, still nearer, close to Thy heart,
> Draw me, my Savior, so precious Thou art;
> Fold me, O fold me close to Thy breast;
> Shelter me safe in that haven of rest.
> Nearer still nearer, Lord to be Thine;
> Sin with its follies I gladly resign;
> All of its pleasures, pomp and its pride;
> Give me but Jesus, my Lord crucified.

Mrs. Morris also wrote the well-known invitational hymn "Let Jesus Come into Your Heart." One Sunday morning after a stirring sermon on repentance, the evangelist gave an altar call. A well-dressed woman walked to the front and knelt at the altar. Lelia followed quietly to assist her. Putting her arm around the woman's shoulders, she said quietly, "Just now your doubting give o'er." The pastor added, "Just now reject Him no more." The evangelist said, "Just now throw open the door." Mrs. Morris added, "Let Jesus come into your heart."

Just that simply was the chorus born, and Mrs. Morris soon had written four stanzas to go with it.

As we close with this hymn, we pray that if anyone here has not yet done as the hymn urges, even now you, too, will let Jesus come into your heart.

Hymn: "Let Jesus Come into Your Heart" (*Sing one or two verses as a congregation.*)

8
July

FOR GOD AND COUNTRY

Invite an Eagle Scout to talk about his experiences while working on his God and Country achievement. This young man's accomplishments will stir up patriotism and spirituality.

Colors: Boy Scouts present colors while all stand.
Salutes to the American and Christian flags: *(Pledges are below.)*
Song: "The Star Spangled Banner"
Speaker: Eagle Scout
Reception: Honor the Eagle Scout and his family. *(Decorate with tiny flags.)*

Pledge to the American Flag
I pledge allegiance to the flag of the United States of America, and to the republic for which it stands, one nation under God, indivisible, with liberty and justice for all.
Pledge to the Christian Flag
I pledge allegiance to the Christian flag, and to the Savior for whose kingdom it stands, one brotherhood uniting all Christians in service and love.

CHRISTMAS IN JULY

This program is designed to stir up missionary interest and procure Christmas gifts for your missionaries. It is necessary to have it early in order for the gifts to reach the mission fields in time for Christmas. Choose one or two families or several single missionaries you know. Books, magazine subscriptions, and music tapes are ideal gifts. Children love books, puzzles, and games. Some missionaries cannot get food items such as gelatin dessert powder, powdered soft drinks, cake mixes, and dry cereals. If postage or import duties for the missionaries are prohibitive, consider sending a gift of money. Whatever you do, remember your missionaries this Christmas. Your love and thoughtfulness will warm their hearts and give them fresh courage.

Ask various ladies to bring Christmas decorations to the church and display them as if it were Christmas. Someone may even have an artificial tree you could decorate, or at least some small ceramic ones. If you have your program in a different place from where you serve refreshments, decorate both places. Put Christmas centerpieces on serving tables.

Play Christmas music as people enter the church to put them into the mood for Christmas.

PROGRAM

Songs: Sing several Christmas carols (*"Joy to the World" is especially appropriate to the missionary theme. Emphasize that your missionaries are spreading this message of joy, and you are going to encourage them by sending them Christmas gifts.*)

Talk: Use a missionary home on furlough, telling about Christmas on his or her field of service and about special opportunities for evangelism during the Christmas season.

Alternative: If you cannot get a missionary speaker, read letters from several missionaries. (*Write to them a few months in advance.*)

Prayer for the Missionary: Be sure prayer requests are mentioned in the letters or talk.

Offering: for Christmas gifts for the missionaries
Song: "Thou Didst Leave Thy Throne"
Refreshments: Serve Christmas cookies with red and green gelatin salads.
Wrap Gifts: If you have bought gifts for the missionaries ahead of time, wrap them together and prepare for mailing.

Note: You may want to have this program for the entire church on a Sunday evening instead of on your usual evening.

9
August

LET'S HAVE A PARTY (SKIT)

Characters: Laura, dressed in a robe, holding a hot water bottle and a thermometer

Five Women, dressed in grays and blacks, each with one of the following signs pinned to her: Self-pity, Pessimism, Grumbling, Resentment, Discontent

Four Women, dressed in bright colors, each with one of the following signs pinned to her: Acceptance, Gratitude, Contentment, Praise.

Laura: *(Takes thermometer out of her mouth and looks at it.)* Look at that—my temperature is 101! No wonder my head aches. *(Sneezes.)* Oh, this is awful! I ache all over. Nobody comes to see me because I'm contagious. I can't go to lunch with the girls today as I had planned. And Don was going to take me to the concert tonight. I'm missing everything. I hate this flu!

(Self-pity, Grumbling, Pessimism, Resentment, and Discontent enter and sit around Laura.)

Laura: Who are you?

Grumbling: I'm Grumbling. Isn't everything awful?

Pessimism: Pessimism here. *(Shakes head.)* Certainly looks bleak, doesn't it?

Resentment: My name is Resentment. Why does this happen to a good person like you?

Discontent: *(Fidgets.)* Discontent. Don't you just *hate* being cooped up like this?

Self-pity: (*Whiny voice.*) And I'm Self-pity. You *poor* thing! I feel so sorry for you!

Laura: Well, thank you, but what are you doing in my bedroom?

Grumbling: You invited us to your party, didn't you?

Laura: Party? What are you talking about? I've got the flu!

Resentment: We know. That's why we're here—for your "pity party."

Laura: (*Looks around at all of them.*) Oh!

Self-pity: (*Heaves a big sigh.*) I'm in charge of the games and such. (*Shuffles some papers.*)

Laura: I just thought of something. I haven't had my devotions yet. I read my Bible every day, even when I have the flu. If you'll excuse me for a few minutes—

(*Visitors exchange glances, then sit back with arms crossed, except for Discontent, who continues to fidget. Laura opens her Bible and begins to read aloud.*)

Laura: "The Lord is my Shepherd." Hmm—that's something. The Lord, the Creator of the universe, is my Shepherd. That means He cares about little old me. That's great! (*Pauses.*) "I shall not want." That means He supplies my needs. Hmm. "He makes me lie down in green pastures." *He* makes me lie down? Did He allow this flu? Do you suppose the green pastures are my Bible and all these other good things I have to read? The Christian radio station? Did He put me here so I could enjoy all this? (*Waves her hand over a stack of magazines and books. Pauses.*) "He leadeth me beside the still waters." Still waters—that's what I need; life has been so hectic lately. It's quiet here in my bedroom. The Lord must have arranged for me to get the flu in order to give me quietness.

(*Laura continues to read silently. Resentment and Pessimism motion to each other and point to Laura, showing signs of impatience and disgust. They finally beckon to each other and slink out.*)

Laura: "He restoreth my soul." Why, I believe He's doing that to me right now! "He leadeth me in the paths of righteousness for His Name's sake."

(*Grumbling gets up and walks out in a huff.*)

Laura: "Yea, though I walk through the valley of the shadow of death, I will fear no evil; for thou art with me; thy rod and thy staff they comfort me."

(Discontent gets up and leaves.)

Laura: "Thou preparest a table before me in the presence of mine enemies." Imagine! "Thou anointest my head with oil; my cup runneth over!" *(Clasps hands and looks up.)*

(Self-pity leaves slowly, reluctantly, with several backward glances.)

Laura: *(Looks around.)* Oh, I've been forgetting my manners. I've neglected my guests, and they're gone! Oh, well, they aren't very good company after all. I can't get enough of this wonderful psalm: "Surely goodness and mercy shall follow me all the days of my life." Tremendous promise! And to top it all, "I will dwell in the house of the Lord forever!" Thank you, Lord, thank you, thank you!

(Acceptance, Gratitude, Contentment, and Praise enter and sit down with Laura.)

Laura: *(Looks up from her Bible.)* Oh, where did you come from?

Acceptance: From the Word of God you're reading.

Laura: *(Looks at Bible.)* Oh, yes, I've been reading the most wonderful verses. But—who are you?

Acceptance: I'm Acceptance. Accepting every circumstance as from a Father's loving hand is the secret.

Laura: Even the flu?

(Acceptance nods.)

Gratitude: I'm Gratitude. "In everything give thanks, for this is God's will for you in Christ Jesus" (1 Thessalonians 5:18).

Laura: Thankful even for the flu, right?

Gratitude: Right!

Contentment: I'm Contentment. "I have learned to be content in whatever circumstances I am" (Philippians 4:11).

Laura: *(slowly)* I'm beginning to feel that way.

Praise: I'm Praise. "I will bless the LORD at all times; His praise shall continually be in my mouth" (Psalm 34:1).

Laura: *(fervently)* Praise the Lord!

Contentment: Thanks for inviting us to your party.

Laura: Party?

Gratitude: Your "praise party."

Laura: Of course! A praise party is so much better than a pity party.

Praise: Ever so much better!

Laura: Welcome, all of you. Please stay all day—all night, too. In fact, you don't have to leave at all—ever!

Praise: Let's start by singing to the Lord, shall we? How about "Allelujah"?

Song: "Allelujah" or some other praise song
Short Prayers of Praise

LET'S GET ACQUAINTED

Do the ladies in your women's group really know each other? Are there new ones coming who need to get acquainted? Try a "Let's Get Acquainted" program to welcome new women and get to know old ones better.

PROGRAM

Opening Songs: "Blest Be the Tie That Binds"
"We Are One in the Spirit"
Scripture Reading: 1 John 4:17-21
Question Time: Divide the group up into twos, being careful not to put two special friends together. Give each lady a piece of paper and pencil. Instruct each one to ask her partner ten questions about herself, writing down the answers. The one who answers will then become the questioner, finding out ten things about her partner. When all are finished, anyone who has anything unusual to report should tell it to the group (with the other person's permission, of course). For instance: "Dee and her husband are in a singing group"; "Marlene takes flying lessons"; "Judy writes poetry"; "Lori's hobby is rosemaling"; "Fran was born in China."

Appropriate questions would be:
1. Where were you born?
2. Are you married?

3. Do you have children?
4. Where did you live before coming to this area?
5. If married, what is your husband's occupation?
6. Do you work outside your home?
7. What are your hobbies?
8. What is your favorite book other than the Bible?
9. What is your pet peeve?
10. What kind of activity gives you the greatest personal satisfaction?

Spin the Bottle: Write the following questions on a chalkboard:
1. What do you usually serve for a company meal?
2. What is your most embarrassing experience?
3. How do you schedule your day in order to get your work done?
4. What are your priorities?
5. Under what circumstances did you become a Christian?
6. What has God been teaching you lately?
7. Do you have a burden you wish to share with the group?

Seat your women in a circle. *(If you have a large group, you may need to break into two or more circles and use a corresponding number of chalkboards, leaders, bottles, and so on.)* The leader stands in the middle of the circle and spins a large soda pop bottle around on the floor. When the bottle stops spinning, its mouth will be pointing at someone in the circle. That person must answer one question of her choice from the board. (You may need a time limit.)

After answering the question, she then spins the bottle to determine who is to answer next. If the bottle points at the same person a second time before everyone has answered once, the person may spin it again or point it at someone of her choice.

Encourage your women to express their thoughts especially on the last three questions. The first four are designed to "break the ice" and get your women talking freely. They are also designed for women in your group who do not have a personal relationship with the Lord or would otherwise be embarrassed to try to answer one of the last three.

Close by joining hands and having a time of prayer for those with special burdens.

10

September

CAMPAIGN FOR KINDNESS

Does the word "kindness" describe all the actions of the ladies in your organization? Sponsor an ongoing program throughout the church year to develop more of the spirit of kindness. Select BYKOTA ("Be ye kind one to another") as your slogan, based on Ephesians 4:32 (KJV).

Kick off the campaign like a political rally. Make a large banner reading "BYKOTA." Stretch it across the front of the room. Prepare placards reading: "Put down the put-downs"; "Cut out the cuts"; "Rout the roast"; "Ban the burn"; "Tame the tongue." Enlist women to "picket the put-down" by interrupting the opening statements of the meeting with a parade through the room, complete with waving placards and chanting the slogans from the placards.

Select three women to "run" for office and make speeches "for" their manner of speech. *(Ideas for speeches follow.)*

Have a campaign collection in reverse. Type verses about kindness on strips of paper. Put those strips in a straw hat with a colorful band reading "BYKOTA." Pass the hat, encouraging women to pull out a verse to memorize to help them win in their own personal campaign for kindness.

Serve popcorn, peanuts, and pink lemonade.

Leader: Calls the meeting to order.

Placard Bearers: "picket the put-down"

Leader: *(Calls meeting to order again.)* One of the first verses we teach our children is: "Be kind one to another." In our world in which insults are so prevalent and supposedly done in fun, it seems we all need to work on being more kind. Adults and children alike need to learn to practice kindness. Our meeting today begins a campaign for kindness. We have several "candidates" who will solicit your votes in this campaign.

Candidate 1: Read Proverbs 31:10-31. Comment briefly on the qualities of the ideal woman. Read again verse 26 and declare that to be her crowning virtue. If she had done all those good deeds described but had done them for praise or in a self-righteous attitude, few would have appreciated her. She might have been labeled a "super mom" by outsiders, but none would rise up to praise her.

Candidate 2: Read Ephesians 4:29-32. Talk briefly about the manner of speech the Lord desires of us, His followers. Point out the implication that kindness is to be followed by forgiveness of the kind that God expresses in forgiving us of our sins through Christ.

Candidate 3: Read James 3:5-10. Talk about how cutting remarks are labeled "friendly insults." How can an insult ever be friendly? Those two words don't go together. Put-downs have also been called velvet darts, but no matter how soft, the barb still cuts, especially if one is already feeling "down" or low in self-esteem.

An ancient torture treatment was similar to what we unwittingly do to our friends and families. The executioner, with a razor, cut one thousand shallow, one-inch-long cuts all over the victim's body. No cut was deep enough to kill, but together the nicks allowed the victim to bleed to death. Cut-downs are verbal razors. Do we really want to cut our loved ones to ribbons so their self-worth seeps away, leaving them wounded and dying personalities?

Leader: BYKOTA stands for the first letter of each of the six little words, "Be ye kind one to another." Let's play a game with our children and each other. Let's tell them the meaning of the word in private, and when we see one another slip into cutting remarks, let's kindly and in love just whisper the word BY-KOTA. Let's launch an all-out "campaign for kindness" in our world.

Pass the Hat: Each woman takes a verse.
Sing as a Prayer: "Let the words of my mouth and the meditation of my heart be acceptable in thy sight, O LORD, my strength and my redeemer." (*If you are not familiar with this verse, Psalm 19:14, as a song, see: Sing 'n' Celebrate! [Waco: Word, 1971], p. 47.*)
Eat and fellowship together

Verses for the Hat
God's kindness to us: Nehemiah 9:17; Psalm 36:7; Psalm 63:3; Psalm 117:2; Jeremiah 32:18; Joel 2:13; Luke 6:35
Encouragement: Deuteronomy 1:38; Deuteronomy 3:28; 1 Samuel 30:6; 2 Samuel 11:25
Exhortation: Acts 11:23; 2 Corinthians 9:5; Titus 1:9; Titus 2:6-9,15; Hebrews 3:13; Hebrews 10:25
Tongue: Job 5:21; Psalm 34:13; Proverbs 10:20; Proverbs 12:18; Proverbs 15:4; Proverbs 18:21; Isaiah 30:27; James 1:26; James 3:5-8; 1 Peter 3:10; 1 John 3:18
(*Use only the number of verses as women in attendance. If you have more women than references given above, you may want to repeat some verses or add some of your own choosing.*)

MISSIONS FAIR

Inform and entertain your church members by having a Missions Fair. You may want to do this in conjunction with your church's annual missions conference. Set up a separate booth for each country in which your church sponsors missionaries, or, if the number of countries is very large, prepare a booth for each area of the world in which you have missions. Feature in the booths: maps, leaflets about the work, curios, costumes, related books (checked out from your church library), letters, posters, pictures (slides, movies, or prints), games, music, and free snacks representative of the countries' foods. Get all the senses involved in this learning experience.

EASY TO PREPARE FOREIGN TASTE TREATS:

Give guests paper plates, and let them wander from booth to booth, sampling the food in each.

From Mexico:

Chilaquiles

For each "nacho" you need: a single corn chip or tortilla chip; a small piece of cheese; and a tiny piece of green chili and/or black olive. Put the cheese and chili or olive piece on the chip and broil until the cheese is slightly melted. Serve warm if possible.

From Portugal:

Sopa de Tomate e Ovos
(Tomato Soup with Eggs)

Heat canned tomato soup. Sprinkle grated, hard-boiled eggs over the soup just before serving. You can serve this in small, paper cups so guests can drink it down or use a spoon.

From Korea:

Pine Seed Honey Cakes

2 cups flour   ½ t. baking powder
1½ T. sesame or salad oil   honey
chopped walnuts and powdered ginger (substitutes for pine seed
    nuts and green ginger)

Sift flour and baking powder. Work in oil by hand until thoroughly mixed. Add honey a little at a time until the dough is the right consistency to roll with a rolling pin to ½ inch thickness. Use the center of a doughnut cutter to cut these small, round cakes. Fry in hot fat about two inches deep. Fry only a few at a time. Dip each cake in honey and drain on paper toweling. Layer the cakes in a dish, sprinkling each layer with nuts and ginger before adding another layer. The cakes are messy to make (dough is sticky), but they keep well and are delicious. Koreans serve them from deep, brass bowls.

From Paraguay:

Sopa Paraguaya
(Corn Bread)

½ cup shortening or oil
1 large onion, chopped
¼ cup water
1 T. baking powder
2 cups cornmeal

5 oz. grated cheese (cream cheese may be used)
1 cup cream style or fresh corn
3 eggs
2 (or more) cups milk·

Sauté onion in fat. Add water and cook slowly. In a mixing bowl, beat eggs and add cheese and corn. Let onions cool a little, then add to egg mix.

Add dry ingredients alternately with milk. Add extra milk if needed, until batter is like cake batter for consistency. Cook in hot oven until golden brown and well cooked in center of pan or skillet (about 30 minutes at 400 degrees). Serves 20 two-inch squares.

From China:

Fried Rice

2 cups chopped onions
4 eggs slightly beaten
6 t. soy sauce
sliced mushrooms
1 T. chopped chives

2 green peppers chopped (optional)
4 cups chopped, cooked meat (chicken, beef, pork, shrimp)
4 cups cold, cooked rice

Brown the onions (and peppers) in small amount of salad oil. Add eggs and stir until slightly set. Remove from pan. Sauté the meat or shrimp in a little more oil. Add soy sauce, seasonings, onion, and rice. When ingredients are thoroughly heated, put in the scrambled eggs and stir. Garnish with chopped chives. Equally delicious hot or cold. Serve with chopsticks.

From Japan:

Tempura

Batter: 1 cup flour   1 egg
       ⅔ to 1 cup water   ½ t. salt

Beat egg well. Add other ingredients to make a batter. Never mind lumps. Dip fish and vegetables in the batter and fry in deep fat. Suggested items: prawns, shrimp, any other kind of fish, green peppers, string beans, carrots, sweet potatoes, onions, greens. Cut vegetables in strips, dip a bunch into batter, and fry. Dip shrimp and pieces of fish into batter and fry. Delicious! Eat with chopsticks or fingers!

From the Philippines:

Buy banana chips from a health food counter. Those are so good, folks may desert potato chips forever.

From Cameroon:

Peanuts, fresh coconut (cut in small pieces)
(Enlist the help of foreign students or refugees to make other foreign snacks.)

Have a missionary speaker or a slide presentation before or after the Missions Fair.

11

October

EMPTY STOMACHS AND CLOSED HEARTS
(A WORLD HUNGER PROGRAM)

PROGRAM

"Feast" Time
Fact Time
Foundation Time
Formula for the Future

"Feast" Time: Plan a real dinner or a symbolic one to get the "feel" of the hungry of this world.

For the dinner: Charge the price of a banquet meal. Let people know ahead of time that they will leave with an empty stomach but an open heart. Serve each person, at plain tables, only ¼ cup cooked rice and a glass of water. "Digest" facts about world hunger. Send the money collected from the banquet tickets to feed the hungry. *(If preferred, take a freewill offering for the hungry instead of selling tickets.)*

For the symbolic meal: Put plain, white paper or cloths on the tables. Put a piece of black construction paper as a placemat for nine settings, and a pretty placemat, candle, and flower at every tenth setting. Make many bundles of ¼ cup raw rice in small plastic bags or wrapping. Make a few bundles of meat, fruit, vegetables, and milk or soda pop (enough for each tenth setting). Put the rice bundles on the black mats and the other bundles on the pretty placemats. Seat women in the darkened room as they arrive, with no preference in seating. Point out that nine out of every ten people in this world exist on ¼ cup of rice daily (if they have even that much), whereas the tenth person has three well-balanced meals each day. Turn the lights on in the room, and enlighten the mind by presenting the facts on the world hunger situation.

Variation: Combine the two ideas above. Serve nine people ¼ cup cooked rice and a glass of water, and every tenth person a meal of meat, vegetables, fruit, beverage, and dessert. Number the places at the table. Let women draw numbers from a hat at the door to find out where they will sit.

Fact Time: (*The following facts may be added to or updated with information you find at the library, from your denomination, or from world relief literature. An additional resource is* Rich Christians in an Age of Hunger, *by Ronald J. Sider. Write the facts on the chalkboard, posters, overhead projector transparencies, or slips of paper to be distributed and read.*)

1. The US makes up only 6 percent of the world's population, but uses almost 40 percent of the world's resources.
2. One-third of the babies in the world die of starvation.
3. Millions exist on an income of less than $40 a year.
4. Each American eats the equivalent of a ton of grain a year, mostly because we eat so much grain-fed meat. This is five times what the average person in developing countries has.
5. In the production of beer and liquor alone, Americans use enough grain to feed 26 million people.

Foundation Time: Ask three women to give the following answers to the question, "Why should Christians feed the hungry?"

A. Read Matthew 4:4. Although it is true that man does not live by bread alone, man must have food if he is to live. Only Christians know the most important need of life, Christ Himself. Only Christians can both give physical bread and introduce people to the bread of life. Secular agencies can distribute food, but they cannot meet the greater spiritual hunger of the masses.

B. The Bible says Christians should feed the hungry. *(Read Deuteronomy 15:11, James 2:15-17, and 1 John 3:17.)* We are told to feed even our enemies. *(Read Romans 12:20.)* To be obedient to the Bible, we must feed the hungry.

C. Jesus says we do service to Him when we feed the hungry. *(Read Matthew 25:35-40.)* He condemned those who refused to feed the hungry. *(Read Matthew 25:41-45.)* To please Christ, we must get involved in feeding the hungry.

Formula for the Future: Ask, "How can we women in this room feed the hungry?" *(Accept all viable answers. Add the following ideas if they are not named.)*

1. Pray for the hungry.
2. Save money by skipping a meal or a treat and fasting on a regular basis. Give the money thus saved to feed the hungry.
3. As an informed citizen, influence government policies dealing with hunger here and abroad.
4. Help the needy in your neighborhood. Supply an ongoing church food pantry. Collect and distribute food at times other than Thanksgiving and Christmas. Hunger doesn't wait for holidays. Check with local agencies to learn of needs you can meet.
5. Develop a simpler life-style so you won't use as much of the world's supply of food and energy, and so you will also have more money to give.

Decide where you will send any funds collected. If your denomination has a hunger and relief fund, channel your money through it so the physical food will be accompanied by the bread of life, Jesus. If you have no such fund, the following are reputable agencies that will forward your money to the hungry of this world. You may know of others.

World Concern
Crista Ministries
19303 Fremont Ave. N.
Seattle, WA 98133

Billy Graham Ministries
Billy Graham Evangelistic Association
1300 Harmon Place
Minneapolis, MN 55403

Compassion International
3955 Cragwood Drive
P.O. Box 7000
Colorado Springs, CO 80933

WOMEN'S DAY OF PRAYER

Many women's groups participate in a world day of prayer. Beautiful plans are distributed annually. If you do not receive the printed programs, use this simple plan for meaningful prayer participation.

Meet at a quiet location, outdoors or inside, and invite women from other churches to join you for prayer. Maintain a spirit of worship. Use taped music if the retreat is outdoors.

For a Come and Go Prayer Session: If the meeting is inside, prepare a prayer room that women can come to and leave at will. Focus on a centerpiece of flowers and a praying hands figurine or picture. On a poster or chalkboard, list Bible verses on prayer to read and prayer requests. Encourage women to add to the list when they come to pray.

For a Longer Prayer Retreat: Jesus recognized the value of retreating to regroup one's spiritual stamina. He went to the mountain to pray. On another occasion He invited His disciples to come apart and rest a while. Prayer retreats aren't necessarily physically restful, but they are spiritually refreshing. The following plan can be adjusted to fit into the time you have allotted for your retreat.

PROGRAM

Quiet Music as Group Gathers
Prayer

74

Get-acquainted Time: Invite women to introduce themselves by saying, "My name is _____, and I praise the Lord for _____."

Special Music: "The Lord's Prayer" (*recorded or live*)

Leader: We have just heard the model prayer Jesus gave His disciples when they asked Him to teach them to pray. Often we call it "the Lord's Prayer." The Bible does record a prayer our Lord prayed for us, His followers. John 17 records the petitions Jesus voiced in our behalf just before going to the cross to purchase our salvation. Please open your Bibles and follow along as I read this prayer for you. (*Read John 17.*) Note especially verse 20. We who gather here today to pray are part of the number who believe in Jesus because of the word spread by His first disciples. We come from a long line of believers and are met here today as one to pray that others might also join the band of believers to one day dwell with Jesus in heaven.

   We will pray together, individually, and in groups.

Prayer Inventory: Distribute these questions. Ask women to prayerfully answer them as quiet music plays.

1. Do I have a regular time each day for personal devotions?
2. Is God real to me when I pray?
3. Do I speak to God on awakening, before I speak to anyone else?
4. Do I pray often throughout the day?
5. Have I learned to be still and listen during my devotional time?
6. Am I completely honest with God when I consider my sins in His presence?
7. Do I turn quickly to God in prayer when I am conscious I have sinned?
8. Do I pray for people who are not in my family?
9. Has anyone I've prayed for ever been saved?
10. Am I willing to work for the fulfillment of my prayers?
11. Can I pray for and with others with whom I disagree?
12. Have I received convincing answers to prayer during the last year?

Have the women pray over their answers and seek to turn the "nos" into "yeses."

Group Prayer: Divide into groups by rows, birthday months, or seasons (if group is small). Select a leader for each group, someone to take prayer requests and guide the prayer time.

Prayer for World Concerns: Assemble again. Show a chart (large enough to be seen by all) of world events needing prayer intervention. Compile and chart information from mission news and general media news about crises in governments, weather, politics, and natural disasters. Discuss the needs, pausing between each for a verbal prayer for that concern.

Individual Prayer: Ask the women to find a quiet spot alone with their Bibles to read and pray for half an hour.

Add music, coffee breaks, prayer testimonies, lunch, and fellowship times as your schedule allows. Remember that prayer is the most important activity at a prayer retreat.

12
November

THANKSGIVING—THANKS-LIVING
(A PRAYER AND PRAISE PROGRAM)

Prepare a center of interest that is lovely and useful as a prayer prompter. Fill a cornucopia to overflowing with fresh or artificial fruits and vegetables. On each piece of fruit, tape a label with the title of one aspect of the fruit of the Spirit listed in Galatians 5:22-23. There are nine of them. If more women are expected, duplicate fruit and labels. At prayer time, give one of the labeled fruits to each woman and ask that she request just this one-word quality for someone she feels led to pray for. Only the prayer leader should pray more than the one word. This technique will help the women who are too timid to pray aloud to conquer their fear. Surely they can read the one-word request while others' eyes are closed.

Make a graffiti sheet by printing "Thank You, Lord, for . . . ." at the top of a long sheet of paper. Tack that to a wall near the room exit.

If you want to change some of the hymns suggested for this program, look in the topical index of your hymnbook for songs about thanksgiving or thankfulness.

Ask the women to bring food to the meeting if your plan is to distribute food baskets to the needy. Put baskets or boxes to be filled on each side of the interest center table.

PROGRAM

Call to Worship: Read Psalm 92.
Sing "Doxology"

77

Leader: We have met to pray to and praise our God at this special time of the year. As Thanksgiving approaches, we will praise our God by singing several of the great songs of thankfulness.

Sing: "Come, Ye Thankful People, Come" (*Sing as a congregation.*)

Fruitful Praying: Distribute the labeled fruit. Read Galatians 5:22-23. Name missionaries and local people in need of prayer. Ask that each woman note the aspect of the Spirit's fruit listed on her labeled fruit and then think of one of the people just named who could use a special measure of that grace. (*Repeat your list of names.*) Explain that in the prayer time, you will reread each name on your list, pausing after each for the women to voice their one-word prayers. Explain that each of the nine words may be assigned to more than one woman (if you have more than nine women at your meeting), but that each woman is still to voice aloud her one-word prayer for at least one of the people named. Your group should feel free to use one-word petitions other than the fruit if they feel so led (for example, "health"). Explain also that it is all right for more than one woman to pray for a particular person, but that each person named ought to be the subject of at least one woman's prayer. You may want to caution your group to be sensitive to the feelings of those present. Close the prayer time with a simple, "Thank You, Lord, for hearing our prayers. Amen."

Ask women to bring their food for the needy to the boxes and return their labeled fruit to the cornucopia while a soloist sings verse 1 of "We Gather Together." The women will join in singing remaining verses when they return to their seats.

Leader: It is a joy to give thanks when all is going well, when we anticipate a great family gathering and a big feast. Thanksgiving once a year is easy. But thanks-living every day? That's another matter. (*Tell the following story, or read it, if you wish, from the book.*)

In *The Hiding Place*, Corrie ten Boom tells of an experience in which she and her sister, Betsie, learned to practice thanks-living in a prison camp. They had been taken as prisoners for hiding Jews from Nazi extermination and were transported to the dreaded Ravensbruck concentration camp in Germany. They had miraculously smuggled in a Bible with them and found it to be their dearest possession as one dreadful day followed another. They were assigned to the large women's dormitory, a gray building designed to house 400 but by then overflowing with 1,400 women. As they first scrambled their way across the filthy, straw-covered platforms that were to be their beds, they discovered other inhabitants besides human beings in the barracks. Fleas! Bloodthirsty fleas everywhere!

Corrie felt they could not bear the place, but Betsie remembered the Bible verses they had read that very morning. (Read 1 Thessalonians 5:14-18.) Betsie declared that the only way they could live there was to follow the Scripture: "Give thanks in all circumstances." So they began to pray. They thanked God for being together, for having the Bible, for the crowded quarters that meant they had more women to witness to, and, at Betsie's insistence, even for the fleas.

Barracks 28 became a holy altar to the Lord as those devout women spoke of the Bible and their faith whenever they were permitted to be indoors amidst their fleas. Strangely, no guard ever came to interfere or take their precious Bible. Daily they thanked God for this unheard of privacy to propagate their faith. Some months later, they learned why no guards came in to stop them from reading and praying with the women. The fleas kept the guards away!

How do you measure up in thanks-living? Can you thank God in *all* circumstances?

Sing: "Count Your Blessings" (*Sing as a congregation.*)
Graffiti Praise: Have the women complete the statement of thanks on the large sheet of paper by the exit. Encourage everyone to read the sheet as they leave after the meeting.
Read as a Poem: "Thanksgiving Hymn." Leader reads verses 1 and 3; women read verses 2 and 4.
Prayer Song: Sing the words "Praise God" over and over to the tune of "Amazing Grace," repeating the phrase until the tune ends.

THE BLIND HYMN-WRITER

This program can be given effectively by the women's group to the entire church if desired. The songs may be sung by the audience or as solos, duets, and so on. After an organ prelude, have a prayer, then turn out the lights in the church, except for a small one for the reader.

PROGRAM

Reader: How would you like to go through life in darkness, not being able to see the beautiful world around you or your friends and family? That was the lot of Fanny Crosby, the blind hymn-writer whose life we will portray for you tonight in word and song. First, let us sing a hymn of praise that she wrote. (*Put on lights.*)

Song: "Praise Him! Praise Him!"

Reader: Fanny Crosby was born in 1823 of humble parents in Southeast, New York. Her eyesight was normal until she was six weeks old, when she contracted a cold that caused inflammation in her eyes. The family doctor being gone, the Crosbys called a strange doctor to attend their baby. This doctor prescribed hot poultices for her eyes. From that time on, her eyesight was so impaired that although she could distinguish between light and darkness at first, eventually she became totally blind.

Although Fanny was blind, she was a happy, normal child. She played with other children, climbed trees, rode horseback, and was full of mischief. She enjoyed the out-of-doors, her special delight being to play with her pet lamb and listen to the gurgling brook. At an early age, she learned to dress herself, comb her hair, and eat neatly.

Fanny's mother and grandmother taught her many things, painting word pictures for her of the stars, birds, and flowers. They also taught her the Bible. As a child, Fanny memorized the first four books of the Old Testament and the four gospels. Later she memorized many other portions.

Although she was blind, Fanny did not feel sorry for herself. When she was eight years old, she wrote this poem:

O what a happy soul am I
Although I cannot see,
I am resolved that in this world
Contented I will be.
How many blessings I enjoy
That other people don't.
To weep and sigh because I'm blind
I cannot and I won't.

Years later Fanny Crosby wrote the words to the hymn "Never Give Up," which reflects her philosophy of life from a Christian standpoint.

Song: "Never Give Up"

Reader: Fanny Crosby was a bright child who longed and prayed for an education. When she was fifteen years old, her prayers were answered; she was sent to the New York Institute for the Blind. Although she was happy to realize her dream at last, Fanny felt lonely her first night at the new school. The matron, a Quaker, said to her gently, "Fanny, I guess thee has never been away from home before."

Fanny answered, "No, Ma'am, and please excuse me, I must cry." After a cry, she felt better and went out to get acquainted with the other girls.

Fanny was delighted to be able to study at school the works of such men as Thomas Moore, Charles Wesley, Longfellow, Tennyson, and Whittier. She read all that she could find that had been put into Braille. Fanny enjoyed English, history, philosophy, and science, but she hated math. Of math she wrote:

Multiplication is vexation
Division is as bad
The rule of three puzzles me
And fractions make me mad.

Fanny loved poetry and music. By the time she was twenty, she was considered a budding poetic genius. She won many friends and honors and became somewhat proud. Dr. Jones, the superintendent of the school, called her into his office one day and admonished her to shun flatterers as she would a viper. He reminded her that any talent she had was a gift from God. Fanny took that admonition to heart and never forgot it. Her humble attitude is seen in the hymns she wrote later, one of which is "Pass Me Not, O Gentle Savior."

Song: "Pass Me Not, O Gentle Savior"

Reader: At the age of twenty-three, Fanny Crosby became a teacher at the New York Institute for the Blind. One winter, cholera struck the city. Fanny volunteered to help nurse the ill and dying. She became so exhausted from her efforts that she was finally forced to take refuge in the country with her students.

During those days, Fanny thought much of death. One night she had a dream in which one of her friends was dying. He asked, "Will you meet me in heaven?" She promised she would, but when she awoke she wasn't sure she was ready for heaven. She had been "religious" all her life, but she was not sure of her salvation. One night when she was attending a revival meeting, the words of a song, "Alas! and did my Savior bleed and did my Sovereign die?" brought light to her soul. She realized that Jesus had paid the price for her sins. She yielded herself completely to the Savior, stood up, and shouted, "Hallelujah!" From that time on, Fanny Crosby's life and talents were dedicated entirely to the Lord; she wrote her poetry to glorify Him. It was no doubt the memory of this experience that caused her to later write a song that has blessed many throughout the years, "Blessed Assurance."

Song: "Blessed Assurance"

Reader: In 1851, Fanny Crosby was inspired to set words to a beautiful melody she heard that had been composed by George Root, music teacher at the school. Together they composed their first cantata.

In 1858, when Fanny was thirty-five years old, she married Alexander Van Alstyne, a blind musician. They had a baby, but it died shortly after birth.

Fanny began writing hymns at the age of forty-one. She felt that at last she had found her true mission in life. For some time she wrote at least three hymns a week, writing over 8,000 altogether in her lifetime. Often the themes for her songs were suggested by publishers or musical composers. Sometimes a musician would play a tune and ask her to write words for it.

One day William H. Doane, hymn composer, said to her, "Fanny, I have a tune I would like you to hear." When Fanny heard it she exclaimed, "That says, 'Safe in the Arms of Jesus!'" Going to her room, she composed the words to that much-loved song in about thirty minutes.

Song: "Safe in the Arms of Jesus"

Reader: Fanny Crosby's prayer was that she might win a million souls to Christ. Only eternity will reveal how many have come to Christ through the hymns she wrote.

Fanny loved to go to rescue missions. One August night when at a mission in New York, she felt led to say that some mother's boy must be rescued that night or perhaps not at all. She invited such a wandering boy to come to the platform after the service. A young man responded to her invitation.

"Do you mean me?" he asked. "I promised my mother I would meet her in heaven, and as I am now living that will be impossible." Fanny had the joy of praying with the young man and hearing him say afterward, "Now I can meet my mother in heaven." That night she wrote the words to "Rescue the Perishing."

Song: "Rescue the Perishing"

Reader: Fanny Crosby never let her blindness make her depressed. Once a minister told her he thought it a pity that the Master who had showered her with so many gifts had not given her sight. Fanny answered that if at birth she had been able to make one request of her Creator, it would have been that she be blind. When the minister expressed surprise, Fanny answered, "When I get to heaven, the first face that shall ever gladden my sight will be that of my Savior." That is alluded to in her beautiful hymn "My Savior First of All."

Song: "My Savior First of All"

Reader: One day at a conference in Northfield, Massachusetts, Dwight L. Moody asked Fanny Crosby for a testimony of her Christian experience. The blind hymn-writer gave her testimony in the words of a hymn she had written that she called her "Soul's Poem," for it expressed the deepest desires of her heart and comforted her when she was troubled.

> Some day the silver cord will break,
> And I no more as now shall sing:
> But, O the joy when I shall wake
> Within the palace of the King!
> And I shall see Him face to face,
> And tell the story—Saved by grace.

Song: "Saved by Grace"

Reader or Pastor: Perhaps tonight there is someone here who, though physically able to see, is blind spiritually. *(Put out lights.)* Your soul is in darkness. In 2 Corinthians 4:3 and 4 we read, "But if our gospel be hid, it is hid to them that are lost: in whom the god of this world hath blinded the minds of them which believe not, lest the light of the glorious gospel of Christ, who is the image of God, should shine unto them" (KJV). Jesus said, "I am the light of the world: he that followeth me shall not walk in darkness, but shall have the light of life" (John 8:12, KJV). Jesus wants to open your spiritual eyes and give you everlasting light.

If you do not have the light of the world in your life, ask Him to come in tonight as we stand and sing in closing one of Fanny Crosby's well-known songs, "Jesus Is Calling."

(Put on lights for closing hymn.)

Song: "Jesus Is Calling"

From Basil Miller, *Fanny Crosby, Singing I Go* (Grand Rapids:Zondervan, 1950), pp. 10-11, 14, 28, 31, 33, 56-57, 59, 68, 77, 94-95, 109.

13
December

THE WORTH OF WOMEN IN WORLD RELIGIONS

This program is designed to help women appreciate more the Christ who elevated them to become joint heirs in His kingdom by focusing on what other religions teach about women.

Select five women to dress in the costumes of the five major world religions—Buddhism, Japanese kimono; Islam, Arab costume; Confuciansim, Chinese dress; Hinduism, Indian sari; Christianity, Western dress. Label five placards with the names of the religions. On the back of each, print the respective statements of belief. Each woman will hold her placard at her side until time for her to speak. As she speaks, she will hold up her card, read the statements on the back, and continue to hold the card up while the next ones are read.

Buddhism: "Just as when the disease called mildew falls upon the field of rice in fine condition, that field of rice does not continue long; just so under whatsoever doctrine and discipline women are allowed, that religion will not last long. Bad conduct is the taint of women. Verily, the life of women is always darkness."

Islam: "Men are superior to women on account of the qualities which God hath gifted the one above the other. Ye may divorce your wives twice; and then either retain them with humanity or dismiss them with kindness. Of other women who seem good to your eyes, take two, or three, or four."

Confucianism: "The Master said, 'Of all people, girls and servants are the most difficult to behave to. If you are familiar with them, they lose their humility. If you maintain a reserve toward them, they are discontented. The woman follows and obeys the man. In her youth she follows her father and elder brother. When married, she follows her son.'"

Hinduism: "With women there can be no lasting friendship; hearts of hyenas are the hearts to women. The husband should not eat in the presence of his wife. Such indeed is the divine ordinance. Women, the low-caste Sundre, the dog, the blow crow, are untruth. Stealing grain, base metals, or cattle, slaying women and low-caste Sundres, and atheism are all minor offenses."

Christianity: "He who created them from the beginning MADE THEM MALE AND FEMALE, and said, 'FOR THIS CAUSE A MAN SHALL LEAVE HIS FATHER AND MOTHER, AND SHALL CLEAVE TO HIS WIFE; AND THE TWO SHALL BECOME ONE FLESH[.]' Consequently they are no more two, but one flesh. What therefore God has joined together, let no man separate" (Matthew 19:4-6). "There is neither Jew nor Greek, there is neither slave nor free man, there is neither male nor female; for you are all one in Christ Jesus. And if you belong to Christ, then you are Abraham's offspring, heirs according to promise" (Galatians 3:28-29).

PROGRAM

Poem: "A Heathen Woman's Face" (*Have this read by a good oral reader.*)

Leader: Much is spoken today of women's liberation. Christ is the liberator of women. We will examine tonight what religions of the world say about women.

Presentation of Religious Views: Women enter, read their placards.

Leader: Christ liberated women to become joint heirs with Him in His kingdom. He walked and talked with women in a culture in which that was not considered proper etiquette. He welcomed their ministering love toward Him. He died for them. He prepares heaven for them so that they might reign with Him in glory. Have you thanked Jesus today for your freedom?

Closing Prayer: Close with a circle of prayer. Sing "Thank You, Lord, for Saving My Soul," or some other appropriate chorus.

A Heathen Woman's Face

Have you ever read the sorrow in a heathen woman's face,
    As you met her eye to eye amid a throng?
She who is by sex your sister, though of different race,
    Have you ever wondered why she has no song?
It will take no occult power to fathom all her secrets deep,
    And it needs no cruel probing just to know;
If you're filled with Christ's compassion and can weep with
      those who weep,
    All her inmost soul will then to you outflow.
If you let Christ's love flow through you with a power she can feel,
    She will follow close behind you as you go;
And if you but turn a moment, you will meet her mute appeal
    For a blessing that your shadow might bestow.
Yes, she feels you bear the comfort she has sought for years to find,
    In the temple, where her gods sit row on row,
And somehow your very presence breathes a balm for troubled
      mind,
    For she feels that you must understand and know.

She's a prisoner that beats against the very bars of life,
    And she longs for death, yet dares not, must not die.
She is cursed with cruel curses should she be a sonless wife,
    And a baby daughter answer cry with cry.
She's the common drudge of yesterday and dreads the cruel
      morrow,
    While today the weary hours drag like a chain.
And she prays to gods all deafened to her tale of sin and sorrow,
    Or if they hear, are heedless of her pain.
She's the daughter of her mother, who before her trod the road.
    She's the mother of a daughter who will know

All the depths of her own anguish, all the heavy, weary load,
    All the bitterness—a heathen woman's woe!
No, 'tis not a heathen woman—'tis a piteous captive throng,
    In the deserts, jungles, paddy fields and marts,
In the lands that know not Jesus, lands of cruelty and wrong,
    Where there is no balm for wounded, aching hearts.
Shall we let this stream flow downward in its widening,
      deathward way?
    Shall we let this flood of misery hold its throng?
We can stem the deadly current if we go and give and pray—
    They must join us in the glad redemption song!

Mrs. W. M. Turnbull
Alliance Weekly

CHRISTMAS SMORGASBORD

Ask each woman (except for guests) to bring her favorite casserole or salad, plus either breads or Christmas cookies. Make lots of coffee and tea to go with this sumptuous meal.

Ladies help themselves at a serving table and sit at long tables covered with festive tablecloths and adorned with Christmas centerpieces.

Variation: Instead of the usual long tables, use square folding tables (borrowed from your ladies), complete with the festive tablecloths and Christmas centerpieces.

PROGRAM

Sing: Christmas carols
Prayer: Thank God for Christmas.

"Quotes on Religions," *Food for the Body, for the Soul* (Chicago: Moody, 1943), p. 97.

"A Heathen Woman's Face," from *Food for the Body, for the Soul* (Chicago: Moody, 1943), p. 103. Used by permission of *The Alliance Witness*.

Panel Discussion: "Where Does Christ Fit into our Christmas Traditions?"

Choose five women, one of them the discussion leader, to be seated in the front, preferably by a table. The leader begins the discussion by asking each of the other four ladies to present information on Christmas traditions.

Leader: Many of our Christmas traditions originated in pagan practices. The birth of Christ came to be celebrated at the same time as the ancient Roman festival heralding the vernal equinox, when the days begin to lengthen, promoting the return of spring. As missionaries took the message of Christmas to the various European countries, the people added their own traditions to the holy holiday. *

Because Christmas became a time of revelry for many, the Puritans banned it when they came to power in England in the 1600s. Town criers went through the streets shouting, "No Christmas! No Christmas!" The early English settlers brought this attitude toward Christmas with them when they established their homes on the shores of our country. The celebration of Christmas was forbidden in early America. People were required to go to work and school as usual. As late as 1870 in Boston, a child who missed school on Christmas Day was severely punished. †

Settlers from Holland, Germany, Ireland, and Scandinavia celebrated Christmas in their new land as they had in their old ones, however. Eventually the stern Puritans also accepted the celebration of Christmas, and it became legal everywhere.

Panel Member One: Christmas Trees

Many years ago, trees were used in religious worship. Ancient peoples decorated trees in honor of their deities. We are told that the origin of the Christmas tree dates back to Martin

---

*Susan Purdy, *Festivals for You to Celebrate* (Philadelphia, New York: Lippincott, 1969), p. 60.

†Elizabeth Hough Sechrist, *Red Letter Days* (Philadelphia: Macrae Smith, 1946), p. 197.

Luther. He supposedly was walking home one snowy evening and saw stars flickering through the branches of a fir tree. To reconstruct the beautiful scene for his family, he cut a small fir tree and decorated it with candles. A candle-lighted tree adorned the Luther home every Christmas from that time on.

In the 1600s, Christmas trees appeared in many German homes. They were decorated with paper flowers, fruits, sweets, and nuts. Gradually candles became popular on Christmas trees, and eventually electric lights. The Christmas tree was introduced by turn to other countries in Europe, and finally to America. Now it has become popular in many other countries as well.

At first the clergy were against the gaily decorated trees, afraid that they would distract their people from the true meaning of Christmas. When the Germans introduced Christmas trees to America, the churches condemned them as "a pagan custom close to idolatry." But eventually the beautiful, lighted evergreen tree was accepted by Christians and non-Christians alike.

In modern times, a lighted Christmas tree sparkles in nearly every home in our country, a silent witness to the Light of the world and the everlasting life He made available to man by coming to earth that first Christmas. It also reminds us of the cross, made from a tree, upon which our Savior bore the sins of the world.‡

Panel Member Two: Christmas Gifts

The first recorded Christmas gifts were brought by the wise men to the Christ child whose birthday we celebrate. They consisted of gold, frankincense, and myrrh.

Today we give gifts to family and friends to express our love and bring happiness. We also do it as a way of honoring Christ. He told His disciples while He was here on earth that what we do for the least of His brethren, we are doing for Him (Matthew

---

‡Susan Purdy, *Festivals for You to Celebrate* (Philadelphia, New York: Lippincott, 1969), p. 75.

25:40). Therefore, when we give gifts to unfortunate people at Christmas, it is as if we are giving a gift to the Savior whose birthday we celebrate.

Panel Member Three: Santa Claus

Santa Claus, surprisingly, has a Christian origin. A young man named Nicholas, who lived during the fourth century A.D., inherited a large sum of money when his parents died. Nicholas, a truly generous soul, shared his money with the poor, always giving his gifts anonymously. One night, as the story goes, he tossed a small bag of gold coins through the open window of a home where the family needed money to pay for a dowry for their daughter. It landed in a stocking drying beside the fireplace. That started the custom of hanging up stockings for gifts on Christmas Eve.

Nicholas became revered as a saint, and his birthday was celebrated each December 6 when children received gifts in his honor. Gradually the birthday of Saint Nicholas merged with the celebration of Christmas. In our country, the revered saint became jolly old Saint Nicholas, or Santa Claus. This Christian man would no doubt be appalled if he could see how many people in the world honor him at Christmas more than they do the Savior. §

Panel Member Four: Christmas Feasting

Feasting during the last days of December dates back to pre-Christian days when people celebrated the birth of the sun after the shortest day of the year had passed. When the celebration of the birth of Jesus merged with this festival, the custom of feasting continued and is still carried on today. Stuffed turkey, ham, potato sausages, lutefisk, oyster stew, eels—each country and each family has its favorite. As for Christmas goodies, the Swiss make gingerbread dolls, the Germans lebkuchen, the Norwegians fattigmand and lefsa, the English plum pudding,

---

§Susan Purdy, *Festivals for You to Celebrate* (Philadelphia, New York: Lippincott, 1969), p. 61.

the Puerto Ricans rice pudding, the Swedish krumkake, and the Americans a great variety of pies and cookies. Feasting has become a very important part of Christmas in America. In many American homes, Christmas means nothing more than feasting and gift-giving.

A discussion of family Christmas traditions will then be carried on by the panel members, with opportunities for the women in the audience to join in. It is interesting to hear how others celebrate Christmas. The leader will then turn the discussion to "Keeping Christ in Christmas," encouraging the panel members as well as the other women to discuss their ideas on having a Christ-centered holiday, giving Jesus Christ His rightful honor. That may include:

- an Advent wreath (lighting one candle at a time each week before Christmas)
- a birthday cake for Jesus, resplendent with candles
- memorizing and singing Christmas carols as a family
- dramatizing the Christmas story
- making a crèche
- taking goodies to shut-ins and the elderly
- bringing lonely people into your Christmas celebration for Jesus' sake
- attending and performing in church Christmas programs and other Christmas services

Closing Song: "Go, Tell It on the Mountain"

14

Plan Your Own Program

SPECIAL SPEAKER

It is permissible and sometimes quite desirable to postpone a planned program so that you can have the privilege of hearing a guest speaker. A steady diet of speakers will hamper your women's creativity and learning experiences, but an excellent speaker from time to time blesses the hearers.

If a missionary or authority in some subject pertinent to the women is coming to town, by all means utilize her. Plan with her as far in advance as possible to develop a good program. Advertise her coming. Encourage her to use slides, curios, maps, and any other visual aids that would enhance learning. Gear any decorations and refreshments to her field, if possible. Pray purposefully for her and her work. Take an offering for her if that is in keeping with your church policies. By all means, pay her enough to cover any expenses incurred plus an honorarium.

CREATE A PROGRAM

Are you the program chairman with no ideas for a program? You can fret, stew, pull your hair, race around the library or bookstores hoping to stumble upon some usable idea; or you can try the following plan.

1. Pray, asking God to guide your thoughts. The Creator is the author of creativity, and He will plant wise ideas when asked (James 1:5).
2. Surround yourself with a Bible that has a good concordance, a dictionary, and your favorite hymnbook.
3. Begin calmly and prayerfully to read the Scriptures. You may begin in the Psalms or some other book that you particularly love. Does a verse suggest a topic the women would profit from studying? Jot down thoughts that come to your mind as you think of the verse and topic.
4. Now thumb through your hymnal. Does a song suggest an idea to you? Look in the topical index for related songs. You may want to build your entire program around hymns. Often a hymn will suggest topics verse by verse.

   Does your songbook identify Scripture verses related to particular songs? Does it have a section of related readings from Scripture?
5. With a topic firmly in mind, look up the key word in a dictionary. Does the detailed definition mention other facets you should investigate? Check those in an encyclopedia.
6. At the end of this creative session, you probably have a verse, a topic, and a song that correlate.
7. Now go to the library and check the topic in the card catalogue. Browse through some books on the subject. If your interest is a current topic, look in the Guide to Periodical Literature to see what is in recent magazines. That resource is particularly helpful if your topic deals with events in countries in which you have a missions interest.

   If you have a program planning committee, ask them to try steps 1 through 5 separately. Then meet together to discuss individual ideas. Each person's creativity will spur the others, and ideas will soon develop. If too many ideas surface, write them down for future programs. (Possible topics: women in the Bible, trust, tears, rearing children, trials, praise.)

   A hymn or verse may suggest a simple visual idea that you could develop into a poster or a center of interest. Use visuals in your programming as much as possible. They stimulate interest and deepen learning experiences.

Other sources that spark program ideas are:

- Christian biographies
- Devotional books
- Poetry books
- Greeting cards
- Napkins with printed messages
- Holiday and seasonal events
- General and church calendars (special days and emphases)
- Paintings
- Newspaper and magazine articles and advertisements (Ads are especially good for slogans.)
- Observing people

For a well-rounded program package, serve refreshments and use decorations related to the season or the program topic. Sometimes you can correlate with both the season and the topic.

The Wright Studio Accessories is an excellent resource for decorative, colorful, and educational aids for meetings with a missions flair. Order a free catalogue from: The Wright Studio, 5638 East Washington Street, Indianapolis, IN 46219. They offer napkins, puzzle mats, favors, program folders, centerpieces, and a wealth of creative ideas to help decorate and educate on most countries of the world. They also feature these topics among others: race; people of special need; urban missions; church; Bible; Christian flags; biblical understanding of missions; peace and reconciliation; justice and human rights; ecology and technology; affluence and poverty; and communicating the gospel.

Let friends know what your subject is, and invite them to supplement the learning experience with curios, mementos, and experiences they may have had. The more people involved in the program preparation and presentation, the greater the number who will attend and be edified by your women's meeting.

Now check out your program plan. Does it:
- Inspire?
- Inform?
- Invite action that will minister to someone, solve a problem, or result in spiritual growth or a change in attitude?

If it meets all those criteria, begin enthusiastically to praise God for the plan He has given you, and begin to "put feet" to your prayers and plans.

Prayer and program power to you!

Moody Press, a ministry of the Moody Bible Institute, is designed for education, evangelization, and edification. If we may assist you in knowing more about Christ and the Christian life, please write us without obligation: Moody Press, c/o MLM, Chicago, Illinois 60610.